The Story of Anne Frank

Nina Wegner

Level 2
(1300-word)

はじめに

　ラダーシリーズは、「はしご (ladder)」を使って一歩一歩上を目指すように、学習者の実力に合わせ、無理なくステップアップできるよう開発された英文リーダーのシリーズです。

　リーディング力をつけるためには、繰り返したくさん読むこと、いわゆる「多読」がもっとも効果的な学習法であると言われています。多読では、「1. 速く 2. 訳さず英語のまま 3. なるべく辞書を使わず」に読むことが大切です。スピードを計るなど、速く読むよう心がけましょう（たとえば TOEIC® テストの音声スピードはおよそ 1 分間に 150 語です）。そして 1 語ずつ訳すのではなく、英語を英語のまま理解するくせをつけるようにします。こうして読み続けるうちに語感がついてきて、だんだんと英語が理解できるようになるのです。まずは、ラダーシリーズの中からあなたのレベルに合った本を選び、少しずつ英文に慣れ親しんでください。たくさんの本を手にとるうちに、英文書がすらすら読めるようになってくるはずです。

《本シリーズの特徴》

- 中学校レベルから中級者レベルまで5段階に分かれています。自分に合ったレベルからスタートしてください。
- クラシックから現代文学、ノンフィクション、ビジネスと幅広いジャンルを扱っています。あなたの興味に合わせてタイトルを選べます。
- 巻末のワードリストで、いつでもどこでも単語の意味を確認できます。レベル1、2では、文中の全ての単語が、レベル3以上は中学校レベル外の単語が掲載されています。
- カバーにヘッドホーンマークのついているタイトルは、オーディオ・サポートがあります。ウェブから購入／ダウンロードし、リスニング教材としても併用できます。

《使用語彙について》

レベル1：中学校で学習する単語約1000語

レベル2：レベル1の単語＋使用頻度の高い単語約300語

レベル3：レベル1の単語＋使用頻度の高い単語約600語

レベル4：レベル1の単語＋使用頻度の高い単語約1000語

レベル5：語彙制限なし

Contents

Introduction 3
Anne's Family 5
Anne the Talker 8
The Rise of the Nazis 12
A New Life 15
Little Women 20
More Friends, More Success 23
Hitler Starts a War 25
Anne the Writer 28
Hitler Takes Holland 32
Anne and Boys 37
Changes in the Frank Family 40
Anne's Diary 44
Margot Gets Called 47
The Franks Disappear 51
The Secret Annex 54
Life in Hiding 56
The van Pels Family 62
Fritz Pfeffer Joins 65
The War Continues 68
Anne as a Teenager 71
More Troubles 77
Discovery 80
Life in Westerbork 87
Auschwitz-Birkenau 90
Bergen-Belsen 97
Anne the Woman 101

Word List 108

読み始める前に

本書で使われている用語です。わからない語は巻末のワードリストで確認しましょう。

- ☐ attic
- ☐ Jews
- ☐ touching
- ☐ religion
- ☐ blame
- ☐ harass
- ☐ mean
- ☐ similar
- ☐ hurt
- ☐ cousin
- ☐ suffer
- ☐ money-hungry
- ☐ worse
- ☐ hateful
- ☐ secretary
- ☐ lively
- ☐ whistle
- ☐ confident
- ☐ math
- ☐ bomb
- ☐ murder
- ☐ sadly
- ☐ slave
- ☐ hidden
- ☐ annex
- ☐ robber
- ☐ prisoner

登場人物

Annelies Marie Frank　アンネリース・マリー・フランク（アンネ） ドイツ系ユダヤ人の少女。ナチスの迫害から逃れ、2年間の隠れ家生活をした後、収容所へ送られわずか15歳で病死。隠れ家生活中に書いた日記が、戦後、父親の手で出版されベストセラーになった。

Otto Frank　オットー・フランク　アンネの父。アンネと性格があい、とても仲が良かった。ナチスの迫害に耐え、家族でただ一人、戦後生き残る。「アンネの日記」を出版するなど、平和活動もした。Robertローベルト、Herbertヘルベルトの兄がいる。

Edith Frank　エーディト・フランク　アンネの母。アーヘンの出身。25歳でオットーと結婚。JuliusユリウスとWalterヴァルターの2人の兄がいる。

Margot Betti Frank　マルゴット・ベッティ・フランク　アンネの3歳違いの姉。おとなしく、誰からも好かれる。アンネと同様、収容所でチフスにかかり病死。

Kathi　キャシー　フランク家のお手伝いさん。

Stephan and Buddy　ステファンとバディ　アンネの従兄弟たち。

Oma/Omi　オマ、オミ　アンネ姉妹は、母方の祖母をオマ、父方の祖母をオミとよんで慕った。

Miep Santrouschitz　ミープ・ザントロシェッツ　オットーの会社、オペクタの従業員。のちにJan Giesヤン・ヒースと結婚し、ミープ・ヒースとなる。「アンネの日記」を見つけ、戦後まで保管し、生きて帰ったオットーに渡す。

Victor Kugler　ヴィクトール・クーフレル　オットーの会社の従業員。ミープらと共に、フランク家の隠れ家生活をサポートする。

Hanneli Goslar (Lies)　ハンネリ・ホースラル（リース）　アンネの仲良し同級生。

Hermann van Pels　ヘルマン・ファン・ペルス　オットーと共にペクタコン商会をひらく。収容所で死亡。妻のAugusteアウグステも収容所に送られ死亡。

- **Peter van Pels　ペーター・ファン・ペルス**　アンネと同じ年の少年、隠れ家生活をともにし、アンネとも最後には仲良くなる。収容所が解放される3日前に死亡。

- **Johannes Kleiman　ヨハンネス・クレイマン**　会計士。後でオットーの会社の所有者となり、フランク一家をサポートする。

- **Bep Voskuijl　ベップ・フォスキュイル**　ペクタコン商会でタイピストとして働く。

- **Keesing　キーシング**　アンネの学校の先生。アンネのライターとしての才能を見抜く。

- **Jacqueline van Maarsen　ジャクリーヌ・ファン・マールセン**　アンネのユダヤ人中学校での友達。近くに住み、よく互いの家に泊まりに行っていた。

- **Peter Schiff　ペーテル・スヒフ**　アンネの最初のボーイフレンド。

- **Helmuth "Hello" Silberberg　ヘルムート(ヘロー)・シルベルベルグ**　アンネが隠れ家生活に入る前の最後のボーイフレンド。

- **Fritz Pfeffer　フリッツ・プフェファー**　オットーの友人の歯科医、隠れ家に同居する。アンネと同室になり、あまり仲がよくなかったという。

- **Mr. and Mrs. de Winter　ド・ヴィンテル夫妻**　収容所でフランク一家と知り合う。娘のJudyはアンネと同年代で友達になる。

- **Janny and Lientje　ヤニ／リーンチェ・ブリレスレイペル姉妹**　収容所でアンネ、マルゴットと同じ作業をさせられていたユダヤ人姉妹。

用語解説　ユダヤ人とユダヤ教

Jewish rules on food（p.7）　Kosher Foodのこと。Kosherとはヘブライ語で「ふさわしい」「てきとうな」の意味。ユダヤ教に基づいた食事規定で、食べることを禁止されている食材やふさわしい調理方法などが規定されている。

synagogue（p.6）　シナゴーグとはユダヤ教の会堂のことで、聖書の朗読や解説を行う集会所のような場所。ユダヤ人の民族統一の精神的な中心でもある。

Hebrew（p.6）　ヘブライ語は古代、パレスチナに住んでいたヘブライ人（ユダヤ人）の言葉で、旧約聖書もヘブライ語で書かれている。現在イスラエルで使われているのは現代ヘブライ語である。

Jewish holidays（p.19）　ユダヤ人の使う暦法による祝祭日。ユダヤ教において神が世界を創世した日とされる紀元前3761年（西暦）を紀元としている。

Torah（p.25）　トーラー（モーセ五書）はユダヤ教の聖典。旧約聖書の最初の5つの書（創世記・出エジプト記・レヴィ記・民数記・申命記）。

Passover（p.40）　過越の祭り。エジプトに捉えられていたユダヤ人がモーセに導かれてエジプトを脱出し、自由になったことを祝う祭り。ユダヤ暦のニサンの月（3月末から4月初め）の一週間にわたって行われる。ユダヤ人の三大祝節の一つ。

Hanukkah（p.98）　ハヌカとは、キリスト教のクリスマスと同時期に祝われるユダヤ教の行事。紀元前168年頃、ギリシア人支配下にあったエルサレムにある神殿を、武装蜂起して奪回したことを祝う祭り。

用語解説　ナチスの第二次世界大戦

Nazi party（p.3）　ヒトラーを党首とする国民社会主義ドイツ労働者党（ナチ党／ナチス）。1933年に政権を掌握し、独裁政治をはじめる。「反共」「反ユダヤ」「アーリア人至上」「反個人」主義を思想とする。

Holocaust（p.3）　「大虐殺／大惨害」を意味するが、とくにナチスによるユダヤ人大虐殺を指す。「ホロコースト」は、元々はユダヤ教の宗教用語で、全燔祭（ぜんはさい）で獣を丸焼きにして供物にしたことが転じて、全焼死、虐殺を意味するようになった。

Kristallnacht or Crystal Night（p.26）　水晶の夜／クリスタルナハトは、1938年11月9日の夜から10日未明にかけ、ドイツ全土で行われたナチスによるユダヤ人の迫害。割れたガラス窓の破片がキラキラ光っていたことから名付けられた。

Gestapo（p.81）　ゲシュタポは、ナチス時代のドイツの秘密国家警察で、1934年以降は親衛隊(SS)の管轄となる。ヨーロッパ全土で活動し、反ナチスやスパイの摘発、ユダヤ人狩りなどを行い、ヨーロッパ中の人から恐れられていた。

Weteringschans（p.86）　ベーテリングスハンスは、アムステルダムにある拘置所で、アンネは収容所へ送られる前の3日をここで過ごした。

Westerbork（p.86）　ヴェステルボルク収容所。オランダ北東部にある通過収容所。アムステルダム駅から列車で移送された。この収容所でいっしょだったリーンチェ・ブリレスレイペルは、戦後、アンはいつもお母さんから離れなかったと証言している。

Adolf Hitler（p.13, 100）　アドルフ・ヒトラーは1889年オーストリアに生まれた。1921年にナチ党の党首となり、

1933年には首相となる。総統になって後は独裁権を掌握し、隣国への侵略を強行し、ついに第二次大戦を引き起こした。ユダヤ人大虐殺を行い、45年ドイツ降伏直前に自殺。

Joseph Mengele（p.91）ナチスの医師、親衛隊の将校。人体実験のためのユダヤ人の選別を行っていた。21カ月間、アウシュヴィッツ収容所で選別を行い、白衣を着たメンゲレは「死の天使」とも呼ばれた。

Auschwitz-Birkenau（p.90）アウシュビッツ＝ビルケナウ収容所。ポーランド南部オシフィエンチム市（ドイツ語でアウシュビッツ）に建てられたドイツ軍の強制収容所。1943年時には14万人が収容されていた。ユダヤ人大量虐殺が行われたガス室などがある。

Bergen-Belsen（p.97）ベルゲン・ベルゼン収容所はドイツニーダーザクセン州にあった強制収容所。ガス室はなかったが、餓死などの方法で収容者を処分した。

アンネ・フランク関連年表

1914-18	第一次世界大戦
1925.5.12	アンネの両親、オットーとエーディトが結婚
1926.2.16	姉マルゴットが生まれる
1929.6.12	ドイツ、フランクフルトでアンネ生まれる
1933	ヒトラーがドイツ首相となる。フランク一家、ドイツを離れ、アムステルダムへ移住
1934	祖母のところに預けられていたアンネもアムステルダムへ移住
1938.3.12	ヒトラーがオーストリアへ侵攻
1939	オマがアムステルダムにて同居。チェコ、ポーランドへドイツ軍侵攻。第二次大戦始まる

1940.5.10 ヒトラー、オランダへ侵攻
1941 ユダヤ人であることを申告する法律ができる
1942 ユダヤ人は黄色い星を胸につけることが義務づけられる
1942.7.5 マルゴットに収容所行きを命じる手紙が届く
　　 7.6 一家は用意していた隠れ家へ移る
　　 7.13 ペルス一家も同居をはじめる
1943.7.18 アムステルダム北部への爆弾攻撃が激しくなる
1944.8.1 アンネの最後の日記が綴られる
　　 8.4 ナチスが隠れ家にやってくる
　　 8.8 ベーテリングスハンスの拘置所から、ヴェステルボルク収容所へ移送される
　　 9.3 一家全員がアウシュヴィッツ収容所へ送られる。オランダからアウシュヴィッツへ向かう最後の列車だった。
　　 11 アンネ、マルゴット、ベルゲン・ベルゼンの収容所へ送られる
　　 12 ドイツの敗戦色が濃くなる
1945.1 ロシアがポーランドに入ったため、ナチスはアウシュビッツを離れる
　　 2-3 ベルゲン・ベルゼン収容所に移された直後、マルゴットに続き、アンネもチフスで死亡
　　 4.30 イギリス軍によりベルゲン・ベルゼン収容所開放
　　 7 ドイツ軍降伏
1947.6.12 アンネの誕生日には、オランダ語による「アンネの日記」が出版される

The Story
of
Anne Frank

Anne, age 11, at her Montessori school in Amsterdam.

Introduction

Anne Frank was a young Jewish girl who lived and died during World War II. This was a terrible time for Jews living in Europe. During the war, a German political group called the Nazi party killed about six million Jewish people in Europe. Anne and her family were among those killed. This horrific time is called the Holocaust.

Anne was German, but she and her family moved to Holland during the beginning of the Jewish peoples' troubles. She lived in Holland for much of her short life. When she turned thirteen, it was clear that living as a Jew in Holland was no longer safe. Nazis sent Jewish people to terrible places called "concentration camps" every day. At concentration camps,

Jews were either forced to work or killed. To hide from the Nazis, Anne and her family lived secretly in an attic for two years.

Anne kept a diary while she lived in hiding. In it, she wrote about her daily life, her hopes, her dreams, and her fears. Although Anne died when she was fifteen years old, her diary lived on. A friend of the Frank family found Anne's writing and saved it. Now, Anne's diary is famous around the world. It has been translated into sixty-seven different languages. Anne's writing is now an important part of history. It is a very human, very touching account of how life was for Jews during World War II.

Anne's short life is a powerful reminder of this terrible time in history. People around the world hope and believe that stories such as Anne Frank's will keep us from ever making the same mistakes again.

Anne's Family

Annelies Marie Frank was born on June 12, 1929. She was called Anne for short. Anne was born in Germany, in a city called Frankfurt-am-Main. She had one older sister, Margot. Anne's parents were Otto and Edith Frank.

Anne's mother and father were both German Jews. Her father, Otto Frank, came from a rich family. He had two older brothers, Robert and Herbert, and one younger sister, Leni. They all went to good schools. They spoke several languages and played musical instruments. Otto's family lived in a large house with a beautiful garden in Frankfurt. The family had all the best things money could buy.

Otto's family was Jewish, but they did not

pay much attention to religion. Otto did not go to synagogue very often. He did not speak Hebrew, the ancient Jewish language. Instead, Otto's parents taught him to be proud of being German.

When Otto was a young man, he went to work in America for a few years. He worked at Macy's in New York. It was the biggest department store in the world at the time. But when Otto got news that his father died, he returned to Germany.

Back in Germany, Otto and his brothers fought in World War I. His mother and sister also helped in the war. They worked in hospitals helping German soldiers who were hurt.

When Otto was thirty-six years old, he met a shy but kind woman named Edith Holländer. Edith was from the German city of Aachen. Edith was twenty-five years old. She liked art, reading, dancing, and nice clothes. She had two older brothers, Julius and Walter.

Edith also came from a Jewish family. But Edith was more religious than Otto. Her family went to synagogue and followed all the Jewish rules on food.

With time, Otto and Edith fell in love. They were married in Aachen on May 12, 1925. They soon had their first baby, Margot Betti Frank, a healthy girl who was born on February 16, 1926. Three years later, Otto and Edith had their second child, Anne. The happy parents soon found out that Anne and her sister were different in almost every way.

Anne the Talker

Anne Frank was a rather difficult child. She was full of life and wanted to do things her own way. This sometimes caused trouble for other people. Even Anne's birth was long and difficult. When she was born, the nurses were so tired that they wrote "male" by mistake on Anne's hospital record!

Anne was not a quiet baby, like her sister Margot. When Anne was brought home from the hospital, she cried for the first six weeks. From the very start, Anne was not afraid to use her voice to express herself. In time, she turned into a lively girl who liked to talk.

Anne and Margot were like night and day. Margot was clean and quiet, while Anne slept

Anne the Talker

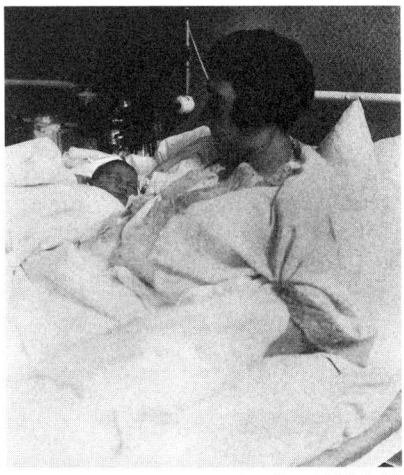

アウシュヴィッツ平和博物館・提供

Anne as a baby, with her mother, Edith, in 1929.

badly and did not always listen to her parents. Kathi, the Franks' housekeeper, called Margot "the little princess." Anne's parents often told Anne to be more like Margot. Sometimes these things made Anne angry, but she was still a happy girl.

Anne was very close with her father. He and Anne were very similar. They both loved to talk and to be with others. Anne was very good at making people laugh. Everyone thought she was full of life—always talking, laughing, and playing. Otto was the only person who could get Anne to go to sleep at night. He told her stories that his mother had told him when he was little. Anne liked this very much and would finally quiet down.

Sometimes Anne's talking would get her into trouble. She said things without thinking first, which sometimes hurt peoples' feelings. But she was such a friendly girl that people did not stay angry with her for long.

Anne was very good friends with her cousins, Stephan and Buddy. Buddy thought Anne was a lot of fun because she was always ready for sports and games. He thought Margot, on the other hand, was more quiet and serious. One of Anne and Buddy's favorite things to do was to dress up in adults' clothes and act like they were famous people.

The Frank girls were also very close with their grandmothers, who they called Oma (Edith's mother) and Omi (Otto's mother).

Anne the Talker

They also loved their aunt and uncles. Edith's brothers, Julius and Walter, didn't have children of their own, so instead, they always played with their nieces and nephews. Margot and Anne loved to spend time with Uncle Julius and Uncle Walter. The girls loved to go for rides in their uncles' car.

The Rise of the Nazis

While Anne was growing up, her country was changing. About ten years before Anne was born, Germany lost World War I. The countries that won the war wanted to make Germany sorry for starting the war. Britain, France, the United States, and a group of other countries made new rules for Germany to follow. One rule was that the German government had to pay a lot of money for the suffering they caused during the war.

These new rules made the German government very weak, which caused a big change in German daily life. Although Germany was a rich country before World War I, losing the war caused many people to lose their money and jobs. And because the German government had no power, it could not help its people. This new way of life made many Germans sad and angry.

Many angry Germans wanted to blame somebody for all the bad things they were experiencing. Just then, a man named Adolf Hitler said he had the answer to all of Germany's problems.

Hitler said that the people to blame were Jews and the German government. If there were no Jews in Germany, and if the country had a new government, then Germany could be a great nation again, he said.

The Jews were an easy group for Christian Germans to blame, because they practiced a different religion and many people did not understand Jewish culture. Soon, Hitler and his new political party, the Nazis, began to grow popular. Some Germans started to harass and hurt the Jewish people in their neighborhood. They called Jews dirty and money-hungry. The country began to be filled with angry talk against the Jews.

In 1930, the Nazi party became the second-biggest political party in Germany. Then, in 1933, Hitler became the Chancellor of Germany. He was now the leader of the entire country.

This caused great change in Germany. Once Nazis started to rule the country, the lives of Jews were more difficult than ever before. Schools, public spaces, and buses became separated between "pure Germans" and Jews. Attacks on Jewish people and Jewish-owned businesses became more common. Many Jews began to leave Germany.

In 1933, when Margot was in second grade, she was told that she had to sit away from the other children in her classroom because she was Jewish. This worried the Frank family very much. They had never experienced this kind of trouble. Otto and Edith decided that Germany was not a safe place to live anymore. They decided to move to Amsterdam, Holland.

A New Life

First, Otto Frank had to go to Amsterdam alone to find work and a house for his family. While he was away, Anne, Margot, and Edith went to live with Edith's mother in Aachen. Anne and Margot loved their Oma. Uncle Walter and Uncle Julius also lived with Oma. They were all happy living together.

But in some German towns, things were getting much worse for Jews. The Nazi party was becoming more powerful. Even German children were supporting the Nazis. German children joined special groups for "pure" German youth. They were taught to shout mean things about Jews. One spring day, Nazis throughout Germany sent a clear message to

Jews. In towns across the country, Nazis went to Jewish businesses and broke windows and wrote hateful messages on the walls.

Next, the Nazi party began to pass laws against Jews. Jewish people lost their jobs and Jewish companies were taken over by the Nazis. It was clear that the Franks needed to leave Germany as soon as they could.

Anne and Margot's aunt, uncle, and cousins Stephan and Buddy moved to Switzerland to escape the Nazis. Stephan and Buddy's father had a successful company in the foods industry. The company was called Opekta. He suggested to Otto Frank that he should open a branch of Opekta in Amsterdam. Otto thought it was a good idea. He found a good building and opened his own Opekta.

On the weekends, Edith went to Amsterdam to help Otto find a place for their family to live. Anne and Margot stayed in Aachen with their Oma and uncles. Finally, Edith and Otto found a nice apartment. The address was 37 Merwedeplein.

A New Life

The apartment was in a new Jewish neighborhood in Amsterdam. Many of the people living there were Jews who left Germany, just like the Frank family. Their apartments were made out of brown brick. The Frank family's home was on the third floor of one of these brick buildings. There was a nice park in the center of the neighborhood where the children could play.

Margot moved into the new home in 1933. Anne stayed with Oma while Margot started school and Otto and Edith got the new house ready. Then, in early 1934, Anne was finally allowed to join her family. She came on Margot's eighth birthday. Edith and Otto put Anne on the table with Margot's other presents as a surprise birthday gift. Anne was four years old.

Otto's business began to do well. Slowly, the Frank family got used to their new life in Amsterdam. They made many friends. One good friend was Miep Santrouschitz (later, after she married, she became Miep Gies), who was Otto's secretary at Opekta. Another good friend was Victor Kugler, who also worked for Otto. Miep and Victor weren't Jewish, but they hated the Nazi party. They would later help the Frank family while they hid from the Nazis.

Margot and Anne liked their new schools. Margot was in the second grade, and Anne started going to a Montessori kindergarten. Edith and Otto both said it was a good choice to send Anne to a Montessori school. Anne always asked many questions and needed a lot of attention. The Montessori system gave her a lot of individual time with her kindergarten teacher, Mr. van Gelder.

Anne and Margot soon learned how to speak Dutch and made lots of friends. Anne became best friends with a girl named Hanneli Goslar. Anne called Hanneli "Lies" (sounds like "Lees"). Lies lived on the ground floor of the Frank family's apartment on Merwedeplein. Anne and Lies did everything together. Sometimes they went to Otto's office and acted like they were secretaries. Because of Anne and Lies's friendship, their families also became very close. The Goslars and the Franks often spent Jewish holidays together.

Even as a new student in a new country, Anne was still full of talk and laughter. She became very popular. But Anne had some trouble at school. She was not very serious about her studies. She had a hard time finishing her work because she wanted to play instead. This was another way she was different from her older sister. Margot was very serious about her studies and was always a good student.

Although Anne was lively, she was not always healthy. She had a weak heart and for a little while, she had to rest every afternoon because of her health problems. However, these things never kept Anne down. She had a bicycle, like most people in Amsterdam. She also learned how to ice skate, and she loved to go to the beach and swim. She even won two swimming awards at the public swimming pool.

Growing up in Amsterdam was a happy time for Anne.

Little Women

Although the Frank family now had a new life in Holland, they still visited their relatives as often as they could. Because of the Nazis, none of the Franks' family members lived in Germany anymore. But the Franks went to Switzerland on their vacations, where Anne and Margot's cousins, Stephan and Buddy, lived.

As she got older, Anne became more interested in fashion and nice clothes. She also liked movie stars. She started collecting pictures of famous Hollywood stars. She and Lies also collected pictures of the children of the royal families of Holland and England.

Anne and her friends liked to keep poetry albums. They wrote poems about their friends and included photos of each other. When the girls went out to play, they called each other by whistling a special song through the mail opening in the front door. Anne couldn't whistle, but that didn't stop Anne. She just sang through the mail opening instead.

Whenever Miep came to the Frank family's house to visit, she noticed that Anne and Margot were growing up quickly. Margot was turning into a very pretty girl, while Anne was very confident. Miep said Anne always talked fast. Both girls had shiny, dark hair. They had it cut in the same short style, no longer than their chin. Both always looked very neat and clean.

Later in life, Lies described how she remembered Anne. She said Anne grew up much faster than other girls. In their group of friends, Anne was the girl who acted older and always knew just what to do. Lies also said Anne was a much better writer than most girls.

In early 1939, Anne's Oma (Edith's mother) came to live with the Franks in their apartment on Merwedeplein. When Oma arrived, Anne was sick in bed. Oma brought Anne a special gift. Anne opened the red box and found a beautiful pen inside. It became her favorite pen, and later, she used this pen to write in her diary.

A few months later, Anne had a special party for her tenth birthday. She invited all her favorite girlfriends. They all wore their best dresses and went to the beach. Otto took a picture of all the girls standing in a line.

But Anne did not spend time just with girls. As she got more popular at school, Anne also became friends with many boys. Lies said that boys always liked Anne. Everyone agreed that Anne was always the center of attention at school and at parties. Already, Anne was becoming a little woman.

More Friends, More Success

Otto Frank loved spending time with his daughters. At the time, it was not very common for a father to spend much time with his children, but Otto gave Anne and Margot a lot of attention. However, Otto Frank was also a businessman. While Edith took care of the girls and the house, Otto had to spend a lot of time at work.

Opekta was doing well. But the company was not making as much money as Otto had hoped. He was trying to find a way to improve Opekta when he met Hermann van Pels.

In 1937, Hermann van Pels moved to Amsterdam with his wife, Auguste, and his son, Peter. Peter was the same age as Margot. The van Pelses were also Jewish. Like the Franks, they had left Germany and come to Holland to escape the Nazis.

Soon, Otto and Hermann became friends. Hermann knew a lot about the food industry, and he went into business with Otto. Hermann and Otto opened a business called Pectacon, which was like a sister company to Opekta. They hired a man named Johannes Kleiman, who became the accountant for both Pectacon and Opekta. Later, Johannes would become a very important person in the Franks' and van Pelses' lives.

Otto also hired an eighteen-year-old woman named Bep Voskuijl. She worked as a typist at Pectacon and soon became friends with the Franks as well. The van Pelses moved into a house near the Franks, and the families became very close. In Amsterdam, the Frank family was surrounded by friends.

Hitler Starts a War

Things were getting worse for Jews in Europe. On March 12, 1938, Hitler's soldiers marched into Austria. Suddenly, German anti-Jewish laws applied in Austria too, and it officially became a Nazi-occupied country. Hitler was preparing for war.

The next year, German troops also entered Czechoslovakia. Then, on November 9 and 10, Hitler ordered attacks on Jews throughout Germany, Austria, and Czechoslovakia. During those two days, 7,000 Jewish businesses were ruined, 191 synagogues were burned, 91 Jews were killed, and 30,000 Jewish men were sent to concentration camps. Nazis burned piles of Torahs (the Jewish holy book) and other

Jewish books. These two days are now known as Kristallnacht, or "Crystal Night" in German, because of all the broken glass from Jewish homes and businesses that covered the streets.

But Hitler was not against just Jews. He also hated blacks, Gypsies, homosexuals, and people who had mental or physical problems. He said these people were useless to society. In 1939, Hitler decided to kill people with mental and physical problems. This would "clean" German society, Hitler said. About 10,000 people with mental or physical problems were taken to a hospital, killed, then burned.

On September 1, 1939, Germany attacked Poland. Hitler had finally started his war.

The Polish army fought hard, but they quickly lost to the Germans. Poland was now under Nazi rule. The Nazis built concentration camps in Poland. One of the most terrible camps was Auschwitz, where hundreds of thousands of Jews went to die.

In Holland, Jews lived in fear of a German attack. Otto wrote to his cousin Milly in England, saying how worried he was about the war. Milly wrote back, suggesting that Otto send Anne and Margot to live with her in England, where they would be safe from the war and the Nazis. Otto soon replied. He thanked Milly, but he said he just couldn't do it. Neither he nor Edith could possibly be separated from the girls. So Anne and Margot stayed in Amsterdam.

Anne the Writer

At the Montessori school, Anne's teacher every year had been Mr. van Gelder. By the time Anne was in fourth grade, he noticed that Anne showed signs of being a good writer. She was always very good at reading and history, and she had good ideas for school plays.

Anne hated math, but she loved to write. As she grew older, her preference started to show more and more. When she was in her first year of high school, she talked so much in math class that she often got in trouble. One day, Mr. Keesing, the math teacher, gave Anne extra work because she was talking too much. He told her to write a paper on people who talk too much. Anne wrote three pages about how

ANNE THE WRITER

talking was a natural female gift. She also wrote that her mother was a person who talked a lot, and that she had passed it down to Anne. When Anne turned in her paper to Mr. Keesing, he had a good laugh and forgave her.

But Anne kept talking in math class. So Mr. Keesing gave her another paper to write. Anne turned it in and stayed out of trouble for two days. But finally, Anne's talking got her into

アウシュヴィッツ平和博物館・提供

Anne (second from left) poses with her friends on her tenth birthday.

trouble yet again. Mr. Keesing told her to write a third paper about people who could not stay out of trouble because they couldn't stop talking. With the help of her friend, Anne wrote a funny poem about three little ducks that were bitten to death by their father because they could not stop quacking. Mr. Keesing laughed hard at this and liked the poem so much that he read it to the class. From then on, Anne and Mr. Keesing became friends. This was the power of Anne's writing.

Years later, after the war, Anne's cousin Buddy said he was very surprised to read Anne's diary. He always knew Anne to be a lively, friendly girl, but he never knew she had a gift for writing. This was a side of Anne that surprised many people. Who knew that under all her laughter and jokes, Anne was also a deep thinker?

In early 1940, Anne and Margot started to write to two pen pals in America. Anne's pen pal was Juanita Wagner, a girl who was Anne's age. She lived on a farm in the state of Iowa.

In her first letter to Juanita, Anne wrote that she was in the fifth grade, that she went to a Montessori school, and that her grandmother lived with her at home. Anne included a picture of Amsterdam. She said she collected picture cards and that she had about eight hundred. She asked Juanita to send a photograph of herself. Anne wrote the letter in Dutch, but Edith or Otto translated it into English so Juanita could read it.

Sadly, this was the only letter Juanita ever received from Anne. Juanita thought Anne may have written more letters but they did not make it to America because of the war.

Juanita may have been right, because on May 10, 1940, Hitler's troops attacked Holland.

Hitler Takes Holland

Children were at school on the day Hitler attacked Holland. They were all sent home until it was safe to come to school again.

During the fighting, the Germans said that they would bomb the city of Rotterdam if Holland did not surrender. The Germans gave Holland some time to decide what to do. But two hours before Holland's time ran out, Germany bombed Rotterdam anyway. Holland had no choice but to stop fighting. It only took four days for Holland to surrender and Germany to take over the country.

About 170,000 Jews lived in Holland at the time. After hearing about all the terrible things the Nazis were doing to Jews in Germany,

Poland, and other countries, many people were frightened. Some Jews tried to leave Holland, and some even killed themselves rather than be killed by Nazis.

Yet, for a few months, everything stayed pretty much the same in Holland. After Germany officially took over the country on May 14, 1940, children were allowed to go back to school. Everybody still had enough food, and people were glad that the shooting and bombing that happened during the four days of fighting were over.

However, the first changes came in October 1940. The Nazis passed a law that said Jews could not own businesses. Jewish teachers and public workers lost their jobs. All Jewish businesses began to be taken over by Germans.

With the new law, Otto Frank was not allowed to own Opekta or Pectacon anymore. But he had an idea, and his friends decided to help him. He had Johannes Kleiman take over Pectacon. Then he changed the official papers on Opekta so that Miep's boyfriend,

Jan Gies, was listed as the owner. This way, both companies looked like they were owned by Dutch people, and Otto was able to keep his companies without the Nazis knowing.

Also, Otto moved his businesses to a new address. Opekta and Pectacon moved to 263 Prinsengracht. The new building had a ground floor that was used for the warehouse, and the first floor became offices. The second floor and attics were used for storing goods. There was also a little three-story house attached to the back of the building. This extra house was common among old Dutch buildings. It was called an annex. Otto made the first floor of the annex his private office. The second and third stories were empty.

In 1941, things got worse for Jews in Holland. New laws said that all Jews had to officially tell the government that they were Jewish. This was so the government would know who the Jews were and where they lived. Then, more and more laws made it hard for Jews to have a good life. All Jewish children had to go to a separate Jewish school. Anne cried when she had to say goodbye to one of her teachers, Mrs. Kuperus. This was the first time Anne and Margot could not go to the same school as all their friends. They both had to travel across town to go to the Jewish high school. Anne was in the first year of high school and Margot was in the fourth.

At the Jewish high school, Anne made a new best friend. Her name was Jacqueline van Maarsen, and she lived in the same neighborhood as Anne. They became very close and talked about everything together. Because of the new Nazi laws, Jewish children could not do the fun things they used to do, like go to the swimming pool or the theater. But Anne and Jacqueline started to have movie nights at Anne's house with friends. Jacqueline said Anne still made everything fun, even during those hard times.

In 1942, a new Nazi law forced all Jews to wear yellow stars on their clothes to show publicly that they were Jewish. Wherever they went, they had to wear the star.

Also in 1942, Hitler had a meeting with fifteen of his top officials. From now on, Hitler said, the Nazi party would have a new goal. That goal was to kill every single Jewish man, woman, and child in Europe. Hitler called this plan the "Final Solution." The fifteen officials at the meeting were the Nazi leaders who would be in charge of meeting this goal.

The plan was to send every Jew in Nazi-occupied countries to special camps where they would all be murdered. After the meeting, Hitler's top officials began to carry out the terrible plan.

Anne and Boys

Right before things began to change in Holland for Jews, Anne met a boy. It was August of 1940 and Anne was eleven years old. During that summer, Anne fell in love with a boy named Peter Schiff.

Peter was fourteen years old, and Anne described him as "a very good-looking boy, tall, handsome," with eyes that came to life when he laughed. Peter and Anne spent a lot of time together that summer, holding hands as they walked around town. In her diary, Anne wrote that she was really in love with Peter, and that Peter liked her very much as well.

But Peter and Anne's friendship ended sadly. Peter's friends found out that Anne was only eleven years old. One of them made fun of Peter about it, saying Anne was only a little girl. After this, Peter stopped talking to Anne. Fortunately, Anne was very busy with other friends so she did not stay sad for long.

Anne turned twelve years old on June 12, 1942. She wrote to her grandmother Omi (Otto's mother) in Switzerland about her birthday and how she was doing lately. In the letter, she told Omi about how many of her friends were boys.

Later that year, the Frank family's good friend Miep was married to her boyfriend, Jan Gies. Anne and Otto went to the wedding, and the next day Otto threw a party for the newly married couple at the new office on Prinsengracht. Anne helped at the party by making and serving the food. She wore new clothes and looked very much like a young lady. Miep noticed that Anne was now very interested in boys, as if she were growing up in a hurry.

Anne's last boyfriend before she had to go into hiding was a sixteen-year-old German boy named Hello Silberberg. He lived with his grandmother and grandfather in Amsterdam. He thought Anne was a very pretty, lively girl. He liked her very much, but his grandparents thought Anne, who was thirteen at the time, was too young for him. Hello and Anne dated for several weeks, and Hello seemed to want to have a future with Anne. But sadly, their friendship was cut short when Anne had to go into hiding.

Changes in the Frank Family

The year 1942 also brought another shock for the Frank family. Oma, who had been sick with cancer, died. Oma had lived together with the Franks for years, and Anne and Margot were very sad to lose their grandmother.

That year, the Franks and the van Pelses celebrated the Jewish holiday of Passover together. At the holiday dinner, Otto and Hermann van Pels talked about the future. They were both worried about their families in Holland under Nazi rule. They knew Nazis were sending Jews to camps either to work as slaves or to be killed. Jewish people who tried to escape from Holland were caught by Nazis at the border. The best thing to do, they thought, would be to hide.

Changes in the Frank Family

アウシュヴィッツ平和博物館・提供

The Frank family in Amsterdam, 1941.

Otto thought the empty floors in Opekta's annex would be the perfect place for the two families to live, hidden away from the world. Of course, they would never be able to go outside of the house or to be seen or heard by anyone. In their secret hiding place, the Franks and van Pelses would wait until the Germans stopped killing Jews or lost the war and left Holland.

But Otto's plan would only work if their friends were willing to help. Johannes Kleiman and Victor Kugler would have to take over Opekta and Pectacon. As owners of the business, they would have to take full responsibility for hiding the families. Also, Miep and Bep would have to keep their secret and help bring food and other daily needs to them. This plan would put all of them in danger. Anyone caught helping or hiding Jews were either sent to prison or killed.

Although Johannes, Victor, Miep, and Bep all knew how dangerous it was to hide Jews, they all agreed to help. In the next few months, they began to prepare the second and third floors of the house. Each room was cleaned. They moved in all the goods that the families would need to live. Furniture such as beds, chairs, tables, and desks had to be moved secretly. Johannes had a brother who owned a truck. He moved all the furniture for them at night, when there were no workers in the Opekta and Pectacon offices.

Smaller things, such as kitchen tools, towels,

and soap were easy to bring into the space without anyone noticing. The four helpers covered the windows with paper, so no one could see inside. They worked on the weekends and in the evenings, slowly getting the space ready. The Franks and the van Pelses would be moving in soon. But none of the children were told about this plan. The adults did not want their children to worry, so they kept it a secret for as long as they could.

Anne's Diary

Anne's thirteenth birthday was a special one. On this day, she received the diary that would make her famous years later.

Anne had wanted a diary for her birthday very badly. So, before the day of her birthday, Otto took Anne to a large bookstore near their house to find one. Anne chose a diary with a red-and-white-checked pattern on the cover.

Friday, June 12, 1942, was Anne's birthday. Anne woke up early, at six o'clock. When she went into the living room, she found all her presents waiting for her on the table. There, lying among a bunch of flowers and other gifts, was her diary. She also received a blue shirt, a bottle of grape juice, a puzzle, some books, and

ANNE'S DIARY

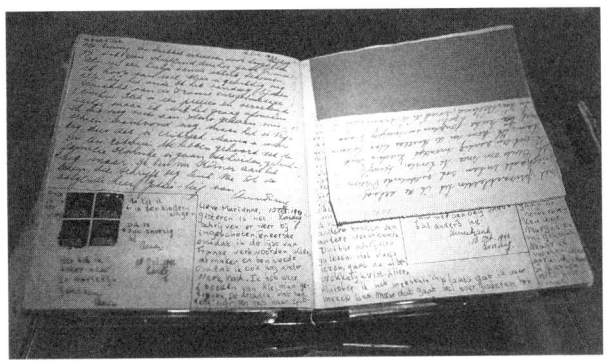

写真提供：ロイター＝共同

Anne's diary is now on display at the Anne Frank House in Amsterdam.

some face cream. When Anne went to school that day, her classmates danced around her in a circle and sang "Happy Birthday."

That day, Anne wrote in her diary for the first time. She wrote, "I hope I will be able to confide everything to you, as I have never been able to confide in anyone, and I hope you will be a great source of comfort and support."

Anne had a birthday party that Sunday, and all her friends came. Anne was very happy to be the center of so much attention. Anne opened more presents, everyone ate strawberry pie, and Otto put on a "Rin Tin Tin" movie. Anne wrote in her diary that her classmates liked the movie very much.

Anne wrote in her diary all the time. Her friends often wondered what she was writing, but she never showed anyone. She covered the page with her hand as she wrote. She named her diary "Kitty" and wrote in it as if she were talking to her closest friend.

Anne also put some photographs of herself in her diary. They were photographs taken in 1940. Most of the black-and-white photos Anne put in her diary showed her smiling or laughing. But one showed her looking quiet and deep in thought. Next to this one, she wrote, "This is a photograph of me as I wish I looked all the time. Then I might still have a chance of getting into Hollywood."

Margot Gets Called

A week after Anne's birthday, school finished and summer vacation started. Anne got her report card for her first year at high school. She did poorly in math, but she did fairly well in other classes and she was satisfied.

Once school was out, Anne spent the first few weeks of vacation going out with friends, seeing her boyfriend Hello, reading, and writing in her diary. It seemed like a normal summer, just like any other. But one Sunday afternoon, something happened that would change the Frank family's life forever.

On Sunday, July 5, 1942, Anne, Margot, and Edith were all at home. Otto was away at a Jewish hospital visiting some patients. At around three in the afternoon, the doorbell rang. Anne was lying in the sun reading a book, and Edith went to answer the door. What Edith found filled her with fear. It was the mailman, delivering a card from the Nazis to Margot. The card gave official orders for Margot to pack her things and go to the train station. She was getting sent to a concentration camp in Germany.

At around this time, thousands of other Jews in Holland also received the card. This was the beginning of Hitler's "Final Solution." Nazi officials had decided to send 4,000 Jews in Holland to concentration camps. Some Jews sent to the camps would work for a while, but in the end, they would all be killed.

If a Jew did not follow the orders on the card, then the Nazis would find that person and send their entire family to the camp. Or, Nazis would come into that person's neighborhood and choose other Jewish families to send instead. It was impossible to escape, because all the borders in Nazi-occupied countries were closed. The only solution was to hide.

Margot Gets Called

Edith and Margot read the card in horror. There was no way Edith would let Margot go to a concentration camp. She knew the entire family had to go into hiding as soon as possible.

Edith rushed off to tell the van Pels family that they had to go into hiding now. Margot went to tell Anne the terrible news.

When Anne found out Margot had received the card, she began to cry. Edith returned home and told Anne and Margot to pack their things as they waited for Otto to come home. During this time, Hello came to the house to see Anne. Edith turned him away, saying Anne couldn't see him at the moment. Hello went home. Sadly, he would never see Anne again.

While the girls packed their things, Anne wondered where they would hide. She did not know that for months, Edith, Otto, and the four helpers at Opekta had been preparing the house behind the office to be their secret hiding place.

The first thing Anne put in her bag was her diary. Then she packed her schoolbooks, some curlers for her hair, her comb, and some old letters. She wrote later in her diary that she was so afraid she could not think clearly.

Finally, at around five o'clock, Otto came home. When Edith told him the news, he jumped into action right away. He called Johannes Kleiman and had him come over that evening. He also had Miep and her husband, Jan, come over. Otto explained to them that Margot had been called up by the Nazis. Everyone was ready to help. Miep and Jan filled their bag and their pockets with clothes, shoes, books, underwear, and anything else they could take with them to the hiding place. Otto wrote a short letter to his family in Switzerland hinting that they had gone into hiding. He could not write where they went because the letter might be found and read by the Nazis. Instead, he just said that he, Edith, and the girls were all together, and that they were safe. That was all.

The plan was set. The Frank family would go into hiding very early the next morning.

The Franks Disappear

Edith woke up the girls at five-thirty. It was a warm, rainy morning. All four Franks wore as many clothes as they could to bring them to the secret hiding place. Anne wore two shirts, three pairs of underwear, two pairs of stockings, a dress, a skirt, a jacket, a raincoat, shoes, a hat, and a scarf.

Margot left first. She rode her bicycle with Miep to the secret hiding place behind the Opekta office. But Anne still had no idea where they were going.

At seven-thirty, Edith, Otto, and Anne also left. Anne's cat Moortje was the only living thing Anne was allowed to say goodbye to. Anne and her parents walked in the pouring rain to the Opekta office, carrying bags full of their things. As they walked, Edith and Otto told Anne where they were going. They told her they had been preparing the empty rooms for months, and they already had plans to go into hiding on July 16. But since Margot was called up by the Nazis, they had to hide now.

When they arrived at the building at 263 Prinsengracht, Miep met them and took them to the rooms that would be the Franks' new home. Margot was there, waiting for them. None of the rooms were organized yet. There were boxes full of things everywhere.

Edith and Margot were in shock and could not move. They lay on two beds while Anne and Otto started to clean and organize things. Thanks to their work, the whole family was able to sleep in clean beds that night.

Back at the Franks' old house, Edith had left a note on her desk to make people think the whole family had escaped to Switzerland. Little by little, news spread around town that the Franks had gone to Switzerland. Anne's friends were very sad, but nobody was very surprised. Since the Nazi call-up cards had started arriving in the mail, many Jewish families were disappearing in the same way.

The Secret Annex

Thousands of Jews went into hiding during World War II. Some hid alone, and some, like Anne, hid with their families. Many parents sent their children away to live with Christian strangers. If the children acted like they belonged to Christian families, they had a chance of surviving the Holocaust.

There were many different types of hiding places. Some people hid in the city and others hid in the country. Farms, empty offices, attics, basements, and even city sewers under the ground were used as places to hide. Anne shared two floors with seven other people for over two years.

The "Secret Annex," as Anne called it, had

three bedrooms, a living room, a bathroom, and an attic. Anne and Margot shared one bedroom on the second floor, and Edith and Otto shared a bedroom next to theirs. A tiny bedroom on the third floor was Peter van Pels's room. Peter's parents, Auguste and Hermann van Pels, slept in the living room.

The living room was also used as the two families' kitchen and dining room. They cooked and ate together, and they spent much of the day together in this one large room. The bathroom was on the second floor, next to Anne and Margot's bedroom.

The door that led to the Secret Annex was hidden by a bookcase. Bep's father built the bookcase especially for the families in hiding.

Although the Secret Annex was small and crowded, Anne felt it was a good hiding place. In her diary, she wrote, "…there's probably not a more comfortable hiding place in all of Amsterdam. No, all of Holland."

Life in Hiding

The Frank family's life in the Secret Annex began on Monday, July 6, 1942. The van Pelses joined them on July 13. At first, everyone was shocked. They couldn't believe how suddenly their lives had changed. Still, the most important thing was that they were safe and together.

At first, Anne described life in the Secret Annex like being on vacation at a strange hotel. To make her room more cheerful, Anne put her pictures of movie stars on the wall. Otto had brought Anne's entire collection from home. But there were many, many rules to follow while living in hiding. Although many people worked at Opekta and Pectacon, absolutely no one aside from the four helpers could know there were Jews hiding in the building. Everyone in the Secret Annex had to be as quiet as possible during office hours. The curtains could never be opened except at night, because the neighbors might see them. Looking out the window was not allowed. The only window that could remain open was the tiny window in the attic. Anne sat by this window often to watch the world outside and to get fresh air.

But that was not all. The bathroom could not be used when anyone else was in the building. All garbage had to be burned every other day so the office workers wouldn't see it. When the Franks first moved in, Margot had a cold, and she was not even allowed to cough. They were always afraid of making any noise that might be heard.

"Not being able to go outside upsets me more than I can say, and I'm terrified our hiding place will be discovered and that we'll be shot," wrote Anne in her diary.

Things were a little easier at night, after all the office workers went home. Then, the families could go into Otto's private office on the first floor and listen to the radio. They tried to listen to the news as much as they could, so they would know what was going on in the war.

Food was also a major source of worry in the Secret Annex. Of course, nobody could go outside so they could not go shopping. They depended entirely on Miep and Bep to bring them food. But because it was wartime, this was not always so easy. Every family in Holland was only allowed a certain amount of food depending on how big the family was. Miep, who only had a husband and no children, had to buy food for all eight people in the annex. She could only do this if she went to a special store where the owner was against the Nazis. The store owner knew Miep was shopping for Jews in hiding, but he never stopped her or reported her to the Nazis.

Miep, Bep, Victor, and Johannes knew they were putting themselves in great danger by helping their Jewish friends. But none of them ever tried to stop helping. Miep came to the annex almost every day to deliver food and other daily needs. "She's also the one who brings five library books with her every Saturday," Anne wrote.

The four helpers visited the Secret Annex at lunch time or after work. On holidays and birthdays, the helpers planned parties and brought gifts. Until the very end, they did everything they could to keep their friends' lives a secret and to help them survive.

One of the most difficult things about living in hiding was not being able to go outside. But another difficult thing was figuring out how to spend the time. When you have to spend every day inside being as quiet as you can, what do you do?

Anne often looked out the window in the attic and watched people go by. "It's really strange watching people walk past," Anne wrote in her diary. "They all seem to be in such a hurry..." Anne longed to move freely again like the people outside. In the annex, she couldn't run, jump, ride her bike, or move her body the way she wanted to. Instead, she practiced dancing, and everyone tried to do as many quiet exercises as possible.

Studying also took up a lot of time. The children tried to keep up with their schoolwork as much as they could so they would not be behind in school when they were finally free. Their parents taught them many subjects, and Bep ordered language courses through the mail for Margot, Peter, and Anne. Anne worked especially hard on learning French. Otto taught her French every day, and Anne tried to help Otto with his Dutch, which he was not very good at. He often made mistakes that made Anne laugh.

Bep gave Margot and Anne office work to do. They did simple work like filing letters and keeping records in a sales book. The work helped Bep, and Anne said it made both Margot and herself feel important.

Everyone in the Secret Annex read a lot to pass the time. They ordered books through Miep, Bep, and the other helpers. The families also bought and played many games.

Anne, of course, spent a lot of time writing in her diary.

The van Pels Family

During the first week of living in hiding, Anne looked forward to the arrival of the van Pels family. She did not know Mr. and Mrs. van Pels's sixteen-year-old son, Peter, very well. She wondered what he would be like.

The van Pelses arrived on July 13, 1942, just a week after the Franks. They settled in, and soon, it was like everyone was part of one big family. But it did not take long for people to start fighting.

Of course, the Franks and the van Pelses respected each other very much. But they lived in a crowded, small space and they had to share everything. It was hard to stay polite in such a situation.

The van Pels Family

At first, there were problems between Edith Frank and Mrs. van Pels. They argued about who should use the bed sheets, the dishes, and other household things. Anne felt Mrs. van Pels was using the Frank family's things without asking first.

Anne also had her own problems with Mrs. van Pels. In her diary, Anne wrote that Mrs. van Pels complained about Anne's manners. She thought that Anne talked too much and that Edith and Otto were not being tough enough on her. This upset Edith, who thought Mrs. van Pels was saying she was a bad mother. Mr. van Pels, too, had things to say about Anne's behavior. All the while, nobody complained about Margot, and Anne felt like she was the only one being picked on. And on and on it went.

Also, at first Anne did not like Peter van Pels very much. Peter was kind, and he was skilled at making things out of wood. But he was very shy and did not talk much. Anne decided that he was not fun to talk to, so she did not pay much attention to him. But slowly, over the course of two years, Anne and Peter became good friends.

Fritz Pfeffer Joins

In November, after four months of living in hiding, the two families decided to invite one more person into the Secret Annex.

The two families had been listening to the radio about the terrible things that were happening to Jews. More and more Jews were getting sent to concentration camps, and others were getting beaten or killed in the streets. They all decided that they had enough room and food in the annex to be able to help one more person. That lucky person would be Fritz Pfeffer, a dentist and friend of Otto's.

Otto sent Miep to visit Mr. Pfeffer and discuss the situation. When Miep met Mr. Pfeffer, she found he was already thinking about going into hiding. Lucky for him, she had a hiding place in mind.

Mr. Pfeffer was very happy for such an opportunity to fall into his lap. He settled his business affairs and moved into the Secret Annex the very next Monday.

Everyone at the Secret Annex was excited about Mr. Pfeffer's arrival. But Mr. Pfeffer did not yet know with whom he would be living. On the day of Mr. Pfeffer's arrival, Miep showed him the secret door to the annex. He was amazed to find a door behind a bookcase. But he was even more amazed when he saw who his new roommates were. When Miep led Mr. Pfeffer into the living room, all the Franks and van Pelses were waiting for him. Mr. Pfeffer was absolutely shocked to see his friend Otto Frank. He thought Otto and his whole family had escaped to Switzerland. Everyone had coffee and wine to celebrate Mr. Pfeffer's arrival.

Anne now had to share her bedroom with Mr. Pfeffer, and Margot moved into her parents' bedroom. At first, Anne was happy that her family was able to help another person. But of course, living in a crowded space with so many people is very difficult. And Mr. Pfeffer had very strong opinions about how a young girl should act. So, within a few months, Anne decided that Mr. Pfeffer was not a pleasant person, and that she did not like sharing her room with him. But she only shared these thoughts with her diary.

The War Continues

The people in the Secret Annex also lived in fear of the war that was going on right around them. Because Holland was occupied by Nazis, British forces were fighting the Germans on Dutch soil.

Although everything was quiet inside the annex, Anne could hear the bombing and shooting happening a few miles away. Sometimes the bombs were so close that they made the house shake, and sometimes the guns were so loud that they sounded like they were right across the street. From the attic window Anne could see airplanes fighting in the sky, and at times the smoke from distant fires would fill up the house. When the shooting and bombing was very bad, Anne would crawl into bed with Otto, and she would feel a little less afraid.

On Sunday, July 18, 1943, the north part of Amsterdam was heavily bombed. Anne wrote in her diary that over two hundred people died and many more people were hurt.

Anne kept an "escape bag" that was packed with some clothes in case the Opekta building was bombed. But even if the Secret Annex was bombed and Anne was forced to run away, she wrote, "being seen on the streets would be just as dangerous as being caught in an air raid."

The two families listened to the radio every day to keep up with the news on the war. Whenever the British and the Allied forces made progress, they became excited and hoped it would finally lead to peace. But whenever the Germans made progress, their hearts sank. Every day, they looked forward to the end of fighting and the moment they could leave their hiding place and step into the fresh air.

For fun, Anne wrote in her diary about the first thing everyone wanted to do when the war ended. Margot and Mr. van Pels wanted a hot bath more than anything, while Mrs. van Pels wanted a cake. Fritz Pfeffer wanted to see his girlfriend, Charlotte, and Edith wanted a cup of real coffee. Otto wanted to visit Bep's father, who had been very helpful but was sick in the hospital. Peter wanted to go downtown. As for Anne, she wrote that she would be so full of joy at being free again that she wouldn't know what to do or where to go. But most of all, she wanted a home of her own and to be able to move around freely again. And, she wrote, she wanted to go back to school.

Anne as a Teenager

When Anne moved into the Secret Annex, she had just turned thirteen. When she came out of hiding, she was fifteen. This means Anne spent her first years as a teenager completely hidden away from the world.

Like many teenagers, Anne did not want to be treated like a child. She felt that she was turning into a woman and she had her own beliefs and opinions. For example, she thought that it was better for women to be strong and to express themselves, rather than to be quiet and weak. In her diary, she often wrote of how she wanted the others in the Secret Annex to respect her and to treat her like an adult. However, Anne was the youngest, and all the adults had something to say about how Anne should improve herself.

Mrs. van Pels often got mad at Anne for talking too much. She also complained to Edith and Otto that Anne had bad manners. But Anne was not the kind of girl who stopped talking just because an adult was mad at her. Instead, Anne told Mrs. van Pels exactly what she thought. Sometimes Anne said things that weren't very nice. At times, this made the others angry with Anne, and at other times they agreed with her. What the others didn't know was that Anne truly wanted to be good, she just didn't know how. She saw herself as a difficult person, and she wrote in her diary about how she wished she could be a girl who the others respected, a girl who didn't talk so much, who was good and nice.

Anne always had a good relationship with her father, even when she was little. When Anne became a teenager, she thought he was the only person who understood her. But Anne and her mother were very different people, and their

Anne as a Teenager

relationship became difficult as Anne grew older.

In her diary, Anne wrote about how she did not feel close with her mother. She thought Edith had no idea who her youngest daughter was. "I'm a stranger to her," Anne wrote. She also felt that Margot was everyone's favorite, especially her mother's. Anne had many fights with her mother while they lived in the annex.

One night, Anne waited in bed for Otto to pray with her and say good night before she went to sleep. Instead, Edith came into Anne's room and told her Otto was busy. "How about if I listen to your prayers tonight?" Edith asked. Anne told her no. Edith began to cry and left the room. For several days after that, Edith could not speak to Anne. Otto was angry with Anne for hurting her mother's feelings. But Anne was not sorry. She felt it was better to be honest about her feelings than to lie to make others happy.

But, as time passed, Anne began to feel differently. She realized that other people's feelings were just as important as her own, and she began to have more respect for Edith, Margot, Mr. Pfeffer, and the van Pelses. Anne was growing up.

As a teenager, Anne's body was also going through changes. She was becoming a woman, and she wrote about these changes in her diary with excitement. She also took good care of the way she looked. She curled her hair every day and tried new hairstyles. She was always happy to receive a new skirt or pair of shoes from Miep, who looked for things on sale for the girls. Anne liked to look good and made sure that her life in hiding did not stop her from taking care of herself.

There were other changes taking place inside Anne. One day, she was surprised to find that she was beginning to have warm feelings for Peter. Of course, at first Anne had not liked Peter very much. Because Anne was such a talker and Peter was not, it seemed as if they had nothing in common. But slowly, Anne began to see good things in Peter, and she realized they were not so different after all. They were both Jewish teenagers who wanted to be free. They both missed the outside world, and they wanted to experience different things and to live life. They both had the same complaints about the adults in the annex, and they both wanted a friend.

It started with little things. Anne gave him a picture of a movie star from her large picture collection. Then she began to help him with his French. Peter told Anne that he wished he were as good at talking as she was. Anne was happy to hear that someone in the annex actually liked how much she talked. Peter began to open up and tell her about himself. They began to have longer talks, and they often sat together by the attic window, watching the world outside.

These little things brought them closer and closer. For a while, Anne thought she was in love with Peter. She was happy to finally have a friend, and the two young people sometimes kissed. But Anne was not sure if she could have a future with Peter, because he was not as deep a thinker as she was. However, once their life in hiding ended, Peter and Anne never got the chance to see where their friendship would go.

More Troubles

As the Franks, van Pelses, and Fritz Pfeffer entered their second year in hiding, life was also becoming more difficult for the world outside. Food and other supplies were running out because of the war, and prices were going up. Many people in Holland could not afford to buy food anymore, so people began to steal.

The Opekta building was broken into several times. Each time a robber entered the building, the people in the Secret Annex shook with fear. What if the robber were to find the secret door that led to their hiding place? Or if the robber didn't find the door, what if the police did? Their life in hidden safety would be over—they would all be sent to concentration camps. But they were lucky. They were never discovered during a robbery.

Food and money began to run out in the Secret Annex, and soon, Anne and the others were eating only potatoes, lettuce, and spinach every day. There was no bread, no butter, no oil, no meat, no milk, no sugar, and no other fruits or vegetables. Sometimes Anne complained in her diary about the terrible food they had to eat, but in the end, she always said food didn't matter as long as they were all alive and safe. But fights became more and more common in the annex. People began to argue over food and to hide what little they had from each other.

The helpers were also dealing with problems of their own. Mr. Kleiman had serious health problems, and Bep's father found out he had cancer. Illnesses spread through Amsterdam because there were no doctors and no food, and both Bep and Miep became sick several times. As the head of Otto's business, Victor Kugler had to deal with the police every time the office was robbed. They had a lot to deal with, but

More Troubles

they did the best they could for their friends in hiding.

Every day, despite arguments, fear, hunger, and other bad feelings, they all listened eagerly for news on the radio. And every day, the British and the Allied forces came closer and closer to entering Holland. Anne and the others waited for the day they would be free—they knew it had to be soon.

On June 6, 1944, news of the Allied forces coming close to victory was all over the radio. American General Dwight Eisenhower said on the radio, "Stiff fighting will come now, but after this, the victory. The year 1944 is the year of complete victory. Good luck!"

This news caused great excitement in the annex. Anne wrote in her diary, "Will this year, 1944, bring us victory? We don't know yet. But where there's hope, there's life. It fills us with fresh courage and makes us strong again." As Allied troops stormed France and moved closer to freeing German-occupied countries, Anne turned fifteen years old.

Discovery

The last time Anne wrote in her diary was August 1, 1944. She wrote an especially deep and thoughtful letter about who she had become over the past two years. During the time she lived in the Secret Annex, she changed from a trouble-making little girl into a thoughtful young woman. But on the morning of August 4, 1944, Nazi officers and members of the Dutch police arrived at 263 Prinsengracht.

Everyone in the Secret Annex was reading or studying, living life as usual. All four helpers were downstairs, doing their normal office duties. Miep, Bep, and Johannes Kleiman were all in the same room. They looked up with shock when the Nazi officers walked in. They knew somebody who knew about the Secret Annex had told the officials. They had been discovered.

A man pointed a gun at the three helpers and told them not to move. The group of men and their leader walked to the back office where Victor Kugler sat. They asked who was in charge of the business. Victor said he was. Then one of the men said, "We know everything. You're hiding Jews and they're in this building. Take us to them."

It was a terrible, sad moment. Victor knew there was no way out, but he still tried his best to fool the Nazis. He got up and led them upstairs to the room with the secret bookcase. He said there was nothing else to see, that this was the last room in the building. However, the group of men shook the bookcase until they found how it opened. The leader pressed his gun to Victor's back and told him to lead them to the Jews.

The first person they met in the annex was Edith. She was alone in her room. Victor now knew it was all over. "The Gestapo are here," he said.

One by one, the group of Nazis found all the other rooms in the Secret Annex and the people hiding in them. Otto and Peter were the last ones to be discovered. They were studying English in Peter's room when a man walked in and pointed a gun at them. He told them to raise their hands over their heads, and they were forced into the next room, where the van Pelses and Fritz were also standing with their arms raised. Then they were all ordered downstairs, where they joined Edith, Anne, and Margot, who stood together silently.

First, the Nazi leader asked Otto to show him where the valuables were. He took the little bit of money and jewelry they had. Then, he asked if anybody had weapons. When they shook their heads "no," he told everyone to get ready. They had five minutes to pack their "emergency bag" with clothes and things they needed. Later, Otto said that Anne never even looked at her diary, which was lying on the floor.

While the families packed their things, the Nazi leader asked Otto how long they had been hiding. When Otto told him two years, he was shocked. "I don't believe you," he said.

Otto showed the Nazi leader the pencil marks on the wall where they measured Anne's height over the years. He showed him some dated letters, and he told the Nazi leader that he had fought as a German soldier in World War I. After this, the Nazi leader began to treat Otto with a little respect. He told his group of men to give the families more time to get ready and to give them space. When everyone had their bags packed, they were led downstairs.

By this time, Johannes had already told Bep to escape, and she was able to leave the office without being seen. Johannes also told Miep to act like she didn't know anything. She agreed silently.

In the private office on the first floor, the Nazi leader asked Victor and Johannes many questions. But the only answer they ever gave was, "I have nothing to say." They were arrested as well and taken to prison with the Franks, van Pelses, and Fritz Pfeffer.

The ten prisoners were taken to a Gestapo (Nazi police) office in South Amsterdam. They were locked into a room with several other prisoners. Otto turned to Johannes and tried to tell him how sorry he was, but Johannes cut him off. He told Otto not to worry.

"It was up to me and I wouldn't have done it any differently," Johannes said.

After some time had passed, Victor and Johannes were taken to another room. Aside from Otto, it was the last time they would ever see the people they had tried so hard to help.

Victor and Johannes were taken to another prison in Amsterdam. A month later, they were transferred to a different camp in Holland. Neither man was ever given a trial.

A week later, Johannes was freed from prison because of his health problems. He returned to Amsterdam and lived there until he died in 1959. Victor, on the other hand, escaped from prison on March 28, 1945. On that day, he and

Discovery

写真提供：ロイター＝共同

Otto Frank and the four helpers at the Opekta office.
From left to right (front row): Miep Gies, Otto Frank, and Bep Voskuijl.
(back row): Johannes Kleiman and Victor Kugler.

other prisoners were being sent to Germany as forced workers. Victor managed to get away. He left Europe for Canada in 1955. He died in Toronto in 1989.

Bep continued to live in Amsterdam until she died in 1983. Miep died on January 11, 2010. She also lived in Amsterdam all her life. Nobody ever found out who called the officials about the Secret Annex.

The day after their arrest, Anne and the others were taken to Weteringschans, another prison in Amsterdam. They stayed there for two days, and on August 8, the eight prisoners were taken to the train station. When they boarded the train, the doors were locked behind them. In the afternoon, they reached Kamp Westerbork, a camp for Jews.

Life in Westerbork

Westerbork was a place where Nazis kept Jews while they figured out what to do with them. This type of camp was called a "transit camp." There was forced work that started at five in the morning. Each week, a list of prisoners' names was announced. The people on the list were those who would be sent to death camps.

When they arrived at Westerbork, the Franks, van Pelses, and Pfeffer were registered. They gave their names and personal information. They were searched for valuables, and then they were sent to their rooms.

The rooms were actually large buildings with many beds in them. There was no privacy or comfort. Because the Franks and their friends had been in hiding, they were sent to special rooms for Jews who broke the law. These Jews were allowed less freedom than everyone else in the camp. The women had to cut their hair short, and the men had to shave their heads. They could not keep their own clothes and had to wear blue uniforms with red cloth on the shoulders. They were not allowed to have soap, they received less food than the other prisoners, and their work was harder.

At Westerbork everyone had to work during the day, but the evenings were free and families were allowed to be together. The Franks made friends with a family named de Winter. Mr. and Mrs. de Winter had a daughter, Judy, who was Anne's age. Anne and Margot also became friends with two sisters, Janny and Lientje Brilleslijper.

The work was hard and there was not enough food. But people were thankful to be with their families, and many felt that the Germans would soon lose the war and they would all be freed.

However, on the night of September 2, 1944, a new list of a thousand prisoners' names was read out loud. The Franks, the van Pelses, and Fritz Pfeffer were all on the list. They prepared for their trip by packing a few things and writing their names on the one blanket that each prisoner was allowed to keep.

At seven o'clock on the morning of September 3, a thousand prisoners came out of their rooms and began to line up outside a train. There were no windows on the train. By eleven o'clock, they had all boarded and were locked inside. This was the very last train to leave Holland for Auschwitz, the largest death camp the Nazis had ever built.

Auschwitz-Birkenau

Inside the train, too many people were packed together and there was no room to move. The Franks and van Pelses sat together. Their train car was full of very sick people. There was one small bucket full of drinking water and one larger bucket to be used as a toilet. There were only a few vegetables and pieces of bread to eat. As the hours passed, the toilet began to smell terrible, and when night fell, it became very cold. During the night, some of the weakest people died.

The train ride lasted three days. On the third night, the train finally arrived at Auschwitz.

When the doors of Anne's train car opened, the prisoners were told to get out and line up as quickly as possible. Men and women were separated and told to stand in different lines. At this point, many families became separated from each other. It was the last time Anne ever saw her father. It was also the last time she ever saw Peter, Mr. van Pels, and Mr. Pfeffer.

Once in line, the Jews' lives were in the hands of the Nazis. Joseph Mengele, the famous Nazi doctor who conducted terrible experiments on Jews, was in charge of choosing who would live and who would die. He walked along the lines of people, separating the people into two groups. Anne, Margot, Edith, and Mrs. van Pels were sent to join the group of women who would live.

It was an hour's walk from the train station to the camp. Anne's group was forced to march to Birkenau, the women's camp at Auschwitz. Their worst fears had come true.

The women were led into a narrow room with showers and told to undress. Their clothes were taken away, and their heads were shaved. They were given grey uniforms. At some point,

Mrs. van Pels got separated in the crowd from Anne, Margot, and Edith.

The women were made to line up again, and one by one, they walked to a desk where they gave their personal information. Their arms were tattooed with their prisoner number. Then they were sent to the building where they would live. Anne, Margot, Edith, Mrs. de Winter, and Judy de Winter were placed in the same building, Block 29. The long, dark room was filled with rows of beds.

Every day, Anne and the women at Birkenau had to wake up at 3:30 a.m. After a poor breakfast, they had to stand outside while the guards called out everybody's names, one by one, to make sure that nobody was missing. After this, the women marched to work, which was half an hour away. Their work was to dig up grass and make piles of dirt. The work did not make any sense, but they had to do it anyway while Nazi leaders and head prisoners shouted at them to work faster. Women who couldn't work were beaten.

At twelve thirty, the women were given a half-hour lunch break. They were given one bowl of watery soup, and they drank this while they sat on the ground. After lunch, the women went back to work until six p.m. Then they were given dinner, which was one slice of bread and a tiny bit of butter. At nine p.m., the women were allowed to go back inside their buildings.

After a while, Anne was chosen to be a building leader's assistant. It was her responsibility to pass out the bread at dinner time. Although she was the youngest girl in the group of assistants, she did her job the best, always giving everyone a fair share of bread.

During all this time, prisoners were continually getting gassed. There were four huge gassing rooms at Birkenau, which were used to murder hundreds of thousands of people. The rooms looked like large shower rooms, with rows of showers heads on the walls. The chosen prisoners were told they had to shower and were forced into the room. Once the doors were locked, the room would be filled with a poison gas. Everyone in the room would die within a matter of minutes. This was the world in which Anne Frank now lived.

One day, there was an announcement that some women would be transferred to a gun factory. Many women wanted to be chosen to go, because there was a bigger chance for survival there than at Auschwitz. Although Judy was taken, Anne, Margot, and Edith stayed at Auschwitz. They weren't chosen because Anne had a skin disease at the time, and the officials did not want any sick prisoners. Although Edith and Margot didn't have the disease, they chose to stay with Anne.

Because of her disease, Anne was sent to the room for sick people. Margot decided to join her, although she wasn't sick. Mrs. Frank worried about her daughters all the time. She didn't eat her daily slice of bread so that she could give it to Anne and Margot. Mrs. Frank looked through the entire camp every day for extra food that she could give to her daughters.

On October 30, 1944, many women at

Auschwitz-Birkenau were gathered together and told to undress. Everyone stood outside, naked, for two days. They were waiting, again, for Dr. Mengele to decide whether they would live or die.

As Mengele made his choices, the women noticed that the old and sick were sent to one side, while the young and healthy were sent to another. They knew then that the sick and old would be gassed, while the young and healthy would live. One by one, Mengele told the women to stand on a scale. Edith and Mrs. de Winter were put into the group with the old and sick. Silently, with fear filling their hearts, the two women watched as Anne and Margot walked up to the scale together. They were thin, naked, and still covered with sores from their skin disease. But they were young and proud and stood straight. Mengele weighed them. He sent them to the young and healthy group.

They would live! But Edith was now separated from her daughters. She cried out, "Oh God, the children!" It was the last time Edith ever saw her daughters.

Edith and Mrs. de Winter were sent to the gas chamber, but another prisoner helped them escape. Although Edith lived for several months after that, without her family she no longer had a reason to live. She died from hunger—and some say a broken heart—on January 6, 1945.

By the end of the year 1944, it was clear the Germans were losing the war. One by one, Nazi-occupied territories were taken over and freed by the Allied forces. The Nazis lost power every day, and they knew that their time was running out. Although they tried to continue the "Final Solution" for as long as they could, they stopped gassing Jews in November of 1944. To cover up their crimes, they destroyed evidence of the mass killings.

The Russians were taking over Poland, and every day they got closer and closer to Auschwitz. In January of 1945, Nazis decided to leave Auschwitz once and for all. They retreated back to Germany, forcing Jewish prisoners into German concentration camps.

Bergen-Belsen

After Anne and Margot survived the gassing selection in Auschwitz, they were put on a crowded train in November 1944. They were headed to Bergen-Belsen, a large concentration camp in Germany. Many prisoners were sent there toward the end of the war.

Anne and Margot survived the cold, four-day trip from Poland to Germany. But when they arrived at Bergen-Belsen, the camp was too crowded. Too many prisoners meant not enough food, not enough water, not enough beds, and worse living conditions than before. With no proper medical supplies, diseases also spread rapidly.

When Anne and Margot arrived at Bergen-

Belsen, they ran into their friends from Westerbork, Janny and Lientje Brilleslijper. When the girls saw each other, they ran into each other's arms and cried. The four girls ended up being assigned to the same building to sleep, where thousands of people had to share one bathroom. Later, Lientje said Anne and Margot would tell stories at bedtime to cheer everyone up.

At Bergen-Belsen, the girls had to work in a shoe factory. They sat at long tables, taking apart old German shoes and putting the good pieces aside for later use. Margot and Janny did well at this job, but Anne and Lientje had to stop working because their hands became infected from the shoes.

Mrs. van Pels also joined Anne and Margot's group when she arrived at Bergen-Belsen at the end of November. The girls were glad to see she was alive, and they tried to stay together as much as they could. In December, their little group celebrated Hanukkah and Christmas together by singing their favorite Jewish songs.

New prisoners were brought to Bergen-

Belsen all the time, and Anne always looked for her friends among the new faces. One day, she found some boys and girls she knew. They told her that her good friend Lies was also at the camp and that they could see each other. Anne became very excited and set up a meeting.

When the two old friends saw each other again, it was through a fence. They both cried and told each other what had happened to their families. They promised to meet each other again, and at the next meeting, Lies brought Anne some food. They only saw each other one other time. Lies became sick, and Anne never saw her friend again.

Soon after, Margot became sick with dysentery and she could no longer get out of bed. Anne stayed with her to take care of her. Janny and Lientje visited them in the sick room to encourage them, but both girls looked very weak.

"We are together and we have our peace," Anne told them.

Then Margot and Anne both caught typhus,

a disease that spread quickly through the camp because of the terrible living conditions. They lay in bed together, in pain and weak, but Anne still got up every day to find Margot and herself something to eat. However, neither sister could hang on to life much longer.

One day, when Janny and Lientje visited Anne and Margot in the sick room, they found Margot lying on the cold stone ground. She had fallen there in her sleep and was not able to get back into bed. Anne told the girls, "Margot will sleep well and when she sleeps, I don't need to get up anymore."

Margot died from the shock of falling onto the floor. Anne was now alone—she lost the only family she had left. A few days later, Anne also died.

Bergen-Belsen was freed by British troops on April 15, 1945, just three weeks after Anne's death.

Adolf Hitler killed himself on April 30, 1945, and the German army surrendered on May 7, 1945. World War II finally came to an end.

Anne the Woman

At the end of the war, the Allied forces and Russians freed thousands of Jewish prisoners. These prisoners were thankful to still be alive, but they had lost their families, their homes, and everything that had been a part of their life. Those who were lucky enough to survive the war now had to start over.

Many people tried to make sense of why these terrible crimes against humanity had happened. Although there were no answers, one thing was certain: A message had to be sent to the world so nothing like this could ever happen again. Many survivors tried to write or record their experiences so people would know exactly what happened during the Holocaust.

Governments all over the world encouraged people to tell the world what had happened. Many first-person stories about World War II were published around the world, and one of them was Anne Frank's diary.

On the day that the people in the Secret Annex were arrested, Miep found and hid Anne's diary. She kept it until the end of the war. Then, when she met Otto Frank again, she gave it to him.

Otto Frank was the only person in the Secret Annex to survive the war. Hermann van Pels was gassed in Auschwitz around November 1944. Auguste van Pels died in 1945, although nobody is sure how she died. Peter van Pels died on March 5, 1945, at a concentration camp in Austria, three days before the camp was freed. Fritz Pfeffer died at Neuengamme concentration camp on December 20, 1944.

Otto was kept at Auschwitz the whole time, and he was still alive when Russian forces freed it. The first thing he did was go back to Amsterdam, asking people about his family the whole way. When he found out that Edith was dead, he put all his energy into finding his two daughters.

When he got back to Amsterdam, the first place Otto went was Miep and Jan's house. They were very happy to see him, and they made enough room in their home for Otto to stay for a while.

It took Otto almost two months to find out about Margot and Anne. But one day, at the Red Cross building in Amsterdam, he found Margot and Anne's names on a list of people who were known to be dead. His heart sank in horror. His family was gone.

When Miep heard from Otto that Margot and Anne were dead, she was heartbroken. But she knew it was the right time to give Otto Anne's diary. Otto couldn't believe Miep had found and kept the precious diary. He took it, but he felt he was not yet strong enough to read it.

Slowly, over the course of several months, Otto read the entire diary. He was shocked and moved to find what a deep, thoughtful woman Anne had become. It was like he was seeing a side of his daughter that he never knew existed. Over the two years Anne lived in hiding, she learned many lessons that girls her age usually don't. Otto saw that Anne was an independent, strong, thoughtful, and kind person, who still loved and believed in humanity, even while she lived through such awful times.

"I still believe, in spite of everything, that people are truly good at heart," she wrote.

Otto shared Anne's diary with his surviving family in Switzerland. Everyone was shocked by it—who knew their talkative little Anne had become such a deep, sensitive woman? And who knew that she was such a good writer? She had such skill, such style, and such a way of describing things so the whole experience of living in hiding really came to life. Otto and his family realized that they had an incredible work on their hands.

From a young age, Anne knew she wanted to be a writer. Otto knew that being published would have made Anne very happy. He decided to send her diary to a publisher.

The first Dutch edition of Anne's diary was published on June 12, 1947, on what would have been Anne's eighteenth birthday. To Otto's shock, the book sold out in six months. The book was then published in Germany, then Japan and France, Britain, and America. People around the world wanted to read Anne's diary. Movies and plays have been made about Anne Frank's life, and every year, school children around the world read Anne's work.

On Wednesday, April 5, 1944, Anne wrote in her diary: "...if I don't have the talent to write books or newspaper articles, I can always write for myself. But I want to achieve more than that...I want to be useful or bring enjoyment to all people, even those I've never met. I want to go on living after my death! And that's why I'm so grateful to God for having given me this gift, which I can use to develop myself and to express all that's inside me!"

Then, she continued: "But, and that's a big

question, will I ever be able to write something great, will I ever become a journalist or a writer? I hope so, oh, I hope so very much, because writing allows me to record everything, all my thoughts, ideals, and fantasies."

At fifteen years old, Anne Frank had no idea that she had already become everything she wanted to be. Although her life was stolen from her, the world will always know her as a strong woman and a great writer who had a message that continues to touch people all over the world.

Sources:

- The Diary of a Young Girl: The Definitive Edition, by Anne Frank (Random House, Inc., New York, 2001)
- Anne Frank and the Children of the Holocaust, by Carol Ann Lee (Penguin, New York, 2006)
- The Anne Frank House Amsterdam (annefrank.org)

Word List

- 本文で使われている全ての語を掲載しています（LEVEL 1、2）。ただし、LEVEL 3 以上は、中学校レベルの語を含みません。
- 語形が規則変化する語の見出しは原形で示しています。不規則変化語は本文中で使われている形になっています。
- 一般的な意味を紹介していますので、一部の語で本文で実際に使われている品詞や意味と合っていないことがあります。
- 品詞は以下のように示しています。

名 名詞	代 代名詞	形 形容詞	副 副詞	動 動詞	助 助動詞
前 前置詞	接 接続詞	間 間投詞	冠 冠詞	略 略語	俗 俗語
頭 接頭語	尾 接尾語	記 記号	関 関係代名詞		

A

- **a** 冠 ①1つの，1人の，ある ②～につき
- **Aachen** 名 アーヘン《ドイツの地名》
- **able** 形 ①《be - to ～》(人が)～することができる ②能力のある
- **about** 前 ①～について ②～のまわりに[の]
- **absolutely** 副 完全に，確実に
- **account** 名 説明，報告，記述
- **accountant** 名 税理士，会計士
- **achieve** 動 成し遂げる，達成する，成功を収める
- **across** 前 ～を渡って，～の向こう側に
- **act** 動 ①行動する ②演じる
- **action** 名 行動，活動
- **actually** 副 実際に，本当に，実は
- **address** 名 住所，アドレス
- **Adolf Hitler** アドルフ・ヒトラー《ドイツの政治家，1889-1945》
- **adult** 名 大人，成人
- **affair** 名《-s》業務，仕事
- **afford** 動《can - 》～することができる，～する(経済的・時間的な)余裕がある
- **afraid** 形 ①心配して ②恐れて，こわがって
- **after** 前 ①～の後に[で]，～の次に ②《前後に名詞がきて》次々に～，何度も～《反復・継続を表す》 after a while しばらくして after all やはり，結局 接 (～した)後に[で]
- **afternoon** 名 午後
- **again** 副 再び，もう一度
- **against** 前 ①～に対して，～に反対して，(規則など)に違反して ②～にもたれて
- **age** 名 ①年齢 ②時代，年代
- **agree** 動 ①同意する ②意見が一致する agree with (人)に同意する
- **air** 名 ①《the - 》空中，空間 ②空気，《the - 》大気 air raid 空襲
- **airplane** 名 飛行機
- **album** 名 アルバム
- **alive** 形 ①生きている ②活気のある，生き生きとした
- **all** 形 すべての，～中 all one's life ずっと，生まれてから all over the world 世界中に all the time いつも，その間ずっと for all ～にもかかわらず once and for all これ

WORD LIST

を最後にきっぱりと 代全部, すべて (のもの[人]) **after all** やはり, 結局 **most of all** とりわけ, 中でも 副まったく, すっかり **all over** ~中で, 全体に亘って, ~の至る所で, 全て終わって, もうだめで

- **allied** 形同盟[連合]した, 関連した
- **allow** 動①許す.《- … to ~》…が~するのを可能にする, …に~させておく ②与える
- **almost** 副ほとんど, もう少しで(~するところ)
- **alone** 形ただひとりの 副ひとりで, ~だけで
- **along** 前~に沿って **walk along** (前へ)歩く, ~に沿って歩く
- **already** 副すでに, もう
- **also** 副~も(また), ~も同様に 接その上, さらに
- **although** 接~だけれども, ~にもかかわらず, たとえ~でも
- **always** 副いつも, 常に **not always** 必ずしも~であるとは限らない
- **a.m.**《A.M.とも》午前
- **am** 動~である,(~に)いる[ある]《主語がIのときのbeの現在形》
- **amazed** 形びっくりした, 驚いた
- **America** 名アメリカ《国名・大陸》
- **American** 形アメリカ(人)の 名アメリカ人
- **among** 前(3つ以上のもの)の間で[に], ~の中で[に]
- **amount** 名量, 額
- **Amsterdam** 名アムステルダム《地名, オランダの首都》
- **an** 冠①1つの, 1人の, ある ②~につき
- **ancient** 形昔の, 古代の
- **and** 接①そして, ~と…②《同じ語を結んで》ますます ③《結果を表して》それで, だから
- **angry** 形怒って, 腹を立てて
- **Anne Frank** アンネ・フランク《ドイツ系ユダヤ人の少女。ナチスの迫害から逃れ, 2年間の隠れ家生活の後, 収容所へ送られる。ベルゲン・ベルゼン強制収容所で死亡。1929-1945》
- **Annelies Marie Frank** アンネリース・マリー・フランク《アンネの本名》
- **annex** 名(建物の)別館, アネックス
- **announce** 動(人に)知らせる, 公表する
- **announcement** 名発表, アナウンス, 告示, 声明
- **another** 形①もう1つ[1人]の ②別の 代①もう1つ[1人] ②別のもの
- **answer** 動①答える, 応じる ②《- for ~》~の責任を負う 名答え, 応答, 返事
- **anti-Jewish** 形反ユダヤ主義の
- **any** 形①《疑問文で》何か, いくつか ②《否定文で》何も, 少しも(~ない) ③《肯定文で》どの~も 代①《疑問文で》何か, いくつか, 誰か ②《否定文で》少しも, 何も[誰も]~ない ③《肯定文で》どれでも
- **anybody** 代①《疑問文・条件節で》誰か ②《否定文で》誰も(~ない) ③《肯定文で》誰でも
- **anymore** 副《通例否定文, 疑問文で》今はもう, これ以上, これから
- **anyone** 代①《疑問文・条件節で》誰か ②《否定文で》誰も(~ない) ③《肯定文で》誰でも
- **anything** 代①《疑問文で》何か, どれでも ②《否定文で》何も, どれも(~ない) ③《肯定文で》何でも, どれでも **anything else** ほかの何か 副いくらか
- **anyway** 副①いずれにせよ, ともかく ②どんな方法でも

THE STORY OF ANNE FRANK

- **apart** 副 ①ばらばらに, 離れて ②別にして, それだけで
- **apartment** 名 アパート
- **apply** 動 適用する
- **April** 名 4月
- **are** 動 ～である, (～に)いる[ある]《主語がyou, we, theyまたは複数名詞のときのbeの現在形》
- **argue** 動 ①論じる, 議論する ②主張する
- **argument** 名 ①議論, 論争 ②論拠, 理由
- **arm** 名 腕
- **army** 名 軍隊, 軍
- **around** 副 ①まわりに, あちこちに ②およそ, 約 move around あちこち移動する walk around 歩き回る, ぶらぶら歩く 前 ～のまわりに, ～のあちこちに
- **arrest** 動 逮捕する 名 逮捕
- **arrival** 名 ①到着 ②到達
- **arrive** 動 到着する, 到達する arrive at ～に着く arrive in ～に着く
- **art** 名 芸術, 美術
- **article** 名 (新聞・雑誌などの)記事, 論文
- **as** 接 ①《as ～ as …の形で》…と同じくらい～ ②～のとおりに, ～のように ③～しながら, ～しているときに ④～するにつれて, ～にしたがって ⑤～なので ⑥～だけれども ⑦～する限りでは 前 ①～として(の) ②～の時 as for ～に関しては, ～はどうかと言うと as if あたかも～のように, まるで～みたいに as usual いつものように, 相変わらず as well なお, その上, 同様に be known as ～として知られている just as (ちょうど)であろうとおり see ～ as … ～を…と考える such as たとえば～, ～のような the same ～ as … …と同じ(ような)～ 副 同じくらい as ～ as one can できる限り～ as ～ as possible できるだけ～ as long as ～する以上は, ～である限りは as much as ～と同じだけ as soon as ～するとすぐ, ～するや否や 代 ①～のような ②～だが
- **aside** 副 わきへ(に), 離れて put aside わきに置く
- **ask** 動 ①尋ねる, 聞く ②頼む, 求める
- **assign** 動 割り当てる
- **assistant** 名 助手, 補佐
- **at** 前 ①《場所・時》～に[で] ②《目標・方向》～に[を], ～に向かって ③《原因・理由》～を見て[聞いて・知って] ④～に従事して, ～の状態で
- **ate** 動 eat(食べる)の過去
- **attached** 動 attach (取りつける)の過去, 過去分詞 形 ついている, 結びついた
- **attack** 動 襲う, 攻める 名 攻撃
- **attention** 名 ①注意, 集中 ②配慮, 手当て, 世話
- **attic** 名 屋根裏[部屋]
- **August** 名 8月
- **Auguste van Pels** アウグステ・ファン・ペルス《アンネ・フランクらとともに隠れ家に同居していた。1900–1945》
- **aunt** 名 おば
- **Auschwitz** 名 アウシュヴィッツ《地名, 強制収容所の名》
- **Auschwitz-Birkenau** 名 アウシュヴィッツ＝ビルケナウ強制収容所
- **Austria** 名 オーストリア《国名》
- **award** 名 賞
- **away** 副 離れて, 遠くに, 去って, わきに get away 逃げる, 逃亡する, 離れる right away すぐに run away 走り去る, 逃げ出す send away 追い払う, 送り出す, ～を呼び寄せる take away ①連れ去る ②取り上げる, 奪い去る ③取り除く turn away 向こうへ行く, 追い払う, (顔を)そむけ

る, 横を向く 形離れた
- **awful** 形 ①ひどい, 不愉快な ②恐ろしい

B

- **baby** 名 赤ん坊 have a baby 赤ちゃんを産む
- **back** 名 ①背中 ②裏, 後ろ 副 ①戻って ②後ろへ[に] get back 戻る, 帰る go back to ~に帰る[戻る], ~に遡る, (中断していた作業に)再び取り掛かる write back 返事を書く 形 裏の, 後ろの
- **bad** 形 ①悪い, へたな, まずい ②気の毒な ③《程度が》ひどい, 激しい
- **badly** 副 ①悪く, まずい, へたに ②とても, ひどく
- **bag** 名 袋, かばん
- **basement** 名 地下(室)
- **bath** 名 入浴, 水浴, 風呂
- **bathroom** 名 ①浴室 ②手洗い, トイレ
- **be** 動 ~である, (~に)いる[ある], ~となる 助 ①《現在分詞とともに用いて》~している ②《過去分詞とともに用いて》~される, ~されている
- **beach** 名 海辺, 浜
- **beat** 動 ①打つ, 鼓動する ②打ち負かす
- **beaten** 動 beat (打つ)の過去分詞 形 打たれた
- **beautiful** 形 美しい, すばらしい
- **became** 動 become (なる)の過去
- **because** 接 (なぜなら)~だから, ~という理由[原因]で because of ~のために, ~の理由で
- **become** 動 ①(~に)なる ②(~に)似合う ③become の過去分詞
- **bed** 名 ベッド, 寝所 be sick in bed 病気で寝ている get out of bed 起きる, 寝床を離れる
- **bedroom** 名 寝室
- **bedtime** 名 就寝の時刻
- **been** 動 be (~である)の過去分詞 助 be (~している・~される)の過去分詞
- **before** 前 ~の前に[で], ~より以前に 接 ~する前に 副 以前に
- **began** 動 begin (始まる)の過去
- **beginning** 動 begin (始まる)の現在分詞 名 初め, 始まり
- **behavior** 名 振る舞い, 態度, 行動
- **behind** 前 ①~の後ろに, ~の背後に ②~に遅れて, ~に劣って 副 ①後ろに, 背後に ②遅れて, 劣って
- **belief** 名 信じること, 信念, 信用
- **believe** 動 信じる, 信じている, (~と)思う, 考える believe in ~を信じる
- **belong** 動 《- to ~》~に属する, ~のものである
- **Bep Voskuijl** ベップ・フォスキュイル《アンネたちの隠れ家での生活を支援していたオランダ人女性。1919-1983》
- **Bergen-Belsen** 名 ベルゲン・ベルゼン強制収容所
- **best** 形 最もよい, 最大[多]の 名 《the -》①最上のもの ②全力, 精いっぱい try one's best 全力を尽くす
- **better** 形 ①よりよい ②(人が)回復して
- **between** 前 (2つのもの)の間に[で・の] between A and B AとBの間に
- **bicycle** 名 自転車
- **big** 形 ①大きい ②偉い, 重要な
- **bike** 名 自転車
- **Birkenau** 名 ビルケナウ《アウシュヴィッツ=ビルケナウ強制収容所のこと》
- **birth** 名 出産, 誕生

- **birthday** 名誕生日
- **bit** 名①小片, 少量 ②《a－》少し, ちょっと
- **bite** 動かむ, かじる 名かむこと, かみ傷, ひと口
- **bitten** 動 bite（かむ）の過去分詞
- **black** 形黒い, 有色の 名黒人
- **black-and-white photo** モノクロ写真
- **blame** 動とがめる, 非難する
- **blanket** 名毛布
- **block** 名（市街地の）1区画
- **blue** 形青い
- **board** 動乗り込む
- **body** 名体
- **bomb** 名爆弾 動～を爆撃する
- **bombing** 名爆撃, 爆破
- **book** 名本, 書物
- **bookcase** 名本箱
- **bookstore** 名書店
- **border** 名国境
- **born** 動 be born 生まれる
- **both** 形両方の, 2つともの 副《both ～ and … の形で》～も…も両方とも 代両方, 両者, 双方
- **bottle** 名瓶, ボトル
- **bought** 動 buy（買う）の過去, 過去分詞
- **bowl** 名どんぶり, わん, ボウル
- **box** 名箱, 容器
- **boy** 名少年, 男の子
- **boyfriend** 名男友だち
- **branch** 名支店, 支社
- **bread** 名パン
- **break** 動①壊す, 折る ②（記録・法律・約束を）破る ③中断する **break into** ～に押し入る, 急に～する 名小休止
- **breakfast** 名朝食
- **brick** 名レンガ
- **bring** 動①持ってくる, 連れてくる ②もたらす, 生じる **bring home** 家に持ってくる
- **Britain** 名大ブリテン（島）
- **British** 形①英国人の ②イギリス英語の 名英国人
- **broke** 動 break（壊す）の過去
- **broken** 動 break（壊す）の過去分詞 形①破れた, 壊れた ②落胆した
- **brother** 名兄弟
- **brought** 動 bring（持ってくる）の過去, 過去分詞
- **brown** 形茶色の
- **bucket** 名バケツ
- **Buddy** 名バディ（・エリアス）《－ Elias. アンネのいとこ, アンネ・フランク財団会長。1925－》
- **build** 動建てる, 確立する
- **building** 名建物, 建造物, ビルディング
- **built** 動 build（建てる）の過去, 過去分詞
- **bunch** 名房, 束, 群れ **a bunch of** 1束の
- **burn** 動燃える, 燃やす, 日焼けする［させる］
- **bus** 名バス
- **business** 名①職業, 仕事 ②商売
- **businessman** 名ビジネスマン, 実業家
- **busy** 形①忙しい ②（電話で）話し中で ③にぎやかな, 交通が激しい **be busy with** ～で忙しい
- **but** 接①でも, しかし ②～を除いて **have no choice but to** ～するしかない 前～を除いて, ～のほかは 副ただ, のみ, ほんの
- **butter** 名バター
- **buy** 動買う, 獲得する
- **by** 前①《位置》～のそばに［で］ ②《手段・方法・行為者・基準》～によっ

て、〜で ③《期限》〜までには ④《通過・経由》〜を経由して、〜を通って 副そばに、通り過ぎて **go by** ①(時が)過ぎる、経過する ②〜のそばを通る ③〜に基づいて[よって]行う

C

- [ ] **cake** 名 菓子、ケーキ
- [ ] **call** 動 ①呼ぶ、叫ぶ ②電話をかける ③立ち寄る **call out** 叫ぶ、呼び出す、声を掛ける
- [ ] **call-up** 名 召集(令)
- [ ] **came** 動 come (来る)の過去
- [ ] **camp** 名 収容所
- [ ] **can** 助 ①〜できる ②〜してもよい ③〜でありうる ④《否定文で》〜のはずがない **as 〜 as one can** できる限り〜
- [ ] **Canada** 名 カナダ《国名》
- [ ] **cancer** 名 癌
- [ ] **car** 名 自動車、(列車の)車両
- [ ] **card** 名 カード、券
- [ ] **care** 名 ①心配、注意 ②世話、介護 **take care of** 〜の世話をする、〜の面倒を見る、〜を管理する **take good care of** 〜を大事に扱う、大切にする
- [ ] **carry** 動 ①運ぶ、連れていく、持ち歩く ②伝わる、伝える **carry out** [計画を]実行する
- [ ] **case** 名 ①事件、問題、事柄 ②実例、場合 ③実状、状況、症状 ④箱 **in case** 〜だといけないので、念のため、万が一
- [ ] **cat** 名 ネコ(猫)
- [ ] **caught** 動 catch (つかまえる)の過去、過去分詞
- [ ] **cause** 動 (〜の)原因となる、引き起こす
- [ ] **celebrate** 動 ①祝う、祝福する ②祝典を開く
- [ ] **center** 名 ①中心、中央 ②中心地[人物]
- [ ] **certain** 形 ①確実な、必ず〜する ②(人が)確信した ③ある ④いくらかの
- [ ] **chair** 名 いす
- [ ] **chamber** 名 部屋、室
- [ ] **chance** 名 ①偶然、運 ②好機 ③見込み
- [ ] **chancellor** 名 (オーストリア・ドイツの)首相
- [ ] **change** 動 ①変わる、変える ②交換する ③両替する 名 ①変化、変更 ②取り替え、乗り換え ③つり銭、小銭
- [ ] **charge** 名 責任 **in charge of** 〜を任せられて、〜を担当して、〜の責任を負って
- [ ] **Charlotte** 名 シャーロッタ(・カレータ)《– Kaletta. フリッツ・プフェファーの恋人。非ユダヤ人。1910-1985》
- [ ] **check** 熟 **check on** 〜を調べる
- [ ] **cheer** 動 ①元気づける ②かっさいを送る **cheer up** 元気になる、気分が引き立つ
- [ ] **cheerful** 形 上機嫌の、元気のよい、(人を)気持ちよくさせる
- [ ] **child** 名 子ども
- [ ] **children** 名 child (子ども)の複数
- [ ] **chin** 名 あご
- [ ] **choice** 名 選択(の範囲・自由)、えり好み、選ばれた人[物] **have no choice but to** 〜するしかない
- [ ] **choose** 動 選ぶ、(〜に)決める
- [ ] **chose** 動 choose (選ぶ)の過去
- [ ] **chosen** 動 choose (選ぶ)の過去分詞 形 選ばれた、精選された
- [ ] **Christian** 名 キリスト教徒、クリスチャン 形 キリスト(教)の
- [ ] **Christmas** 名 クリスマス
- [ ] **circle** 名 ①円、円周、輪 ②循環、軌道 ③仲間、サークル **in a circle** 輪

THE STORY OF ANNE FRANK

になって
- □ **city** 名①都市, 都会 ②《the –》(全)市民
- □ **class** 名①学級, 組, 階級 ②授業
- □ **classmate** 名同級生, 級友
- □ **classroom** 名教室, クラス
- □ **clean** 形①きれいな, 清潔な ②正当な 動掃除する, よごれを落とす
- □ **clear** 形①はっきりした, 明白な ②澄んだ ③(よく)晴れた
- □ **clearly** 副①明らかに, はっきりと ②《返答に用いて》そのとおり
- □ **close** 形①近い ②親しい ③狭い **closer and closer** どんどん近づく 副①接近して ②密として 動①閉まる, 閉める ②終える, 閉店する
- □ **cloth** 名布(地), テーブルクロス, ふきん
- □ **clothes** 名衣服, 身につけるもの
- □ **coffee** 名コーヒー
- □ **cold** 形寒い, 冷たい 名風邪 **have a cold** 風邪を引いている
- □ **collect** 動①集める ②まとめる
- □ **collection** 名収集, 収蔵物
- □ **comb** 名くし
- □ **come** 動①来る, 行く, 現れる ②(出来事が)起こる, 生じる ③~になる ④comeの過去分詞 **come in** 中にはいる, やってくる, 出回る **come into** ~に入ってくる **come out of** ~から出てくる, ~をうまく乗り越える **come over** やって来る, ~の身にふりかかる **come to life** 目覚める, 復活する **come true** 実現する
- □ **comfort** 名①快適さ, 満足 ②慰め ③安楽
- □ **comfortable** 形快適な, 心地よい
- □ **common** 形①共通の, 共同の ②普通の, 平凡な ③一般の, 公共の 名**in common** (~と)共通して
- □ **company** 名会社
- □ **complain** 動不平[苦情]を言う, ぶつぶつ言
- □ **complaint** 名不平, 不満(の種)
- □ **complete** 形完全な, まったくの, 完成した
- □ **completely** 副完全に, すっかり
- □ **concentration camp** 強制収容所
- □ **condition** 名①(健康)状態, 境遇 ②《-s》状況, 様子 ③条件
- □ **conduct** 動実施する, 処理[処置]する
- □ **confide** 動信頼する, 信用する, (秘密などを)打ち明ける
- □ **confident** 形自信のある, 自信に満ちた
- □ **continually** 副継続的に, 絶えず, ひっきりなしに
- □ **continue** 動続く, 続ける, (中断後)再開する, (ある方向に)移動していく
- □ **cook** 動料理する
- □ **cough** 動せきをする
- □ **could** 助①can(~できる)の過去 ②《控え目な推量・可能性・願望などを表す》
- □ **country** 名国
- □ **couple** 名①2つ, 対 ②夫婦, 一組
- □ **courage** 名勇気, 度胸
- □ **course** 名①経過, 成り行き ②**of course** もちろん, 当然
- □ **cousin** 名いとこ
- □ **cover** 動①覆う, 包む, 隠す **cover up** 身をくるむ, すっかり覆う 名覆い, カバー
- □ **crawl** 動はう, 腹ばいで進む, ゆっくり進む
- □ **cream** 名クリーム
- □ **crime** 名(法律上の)罪, 犯罪
- □ **crowd** 名群集, 雑踏, 多数, 聴衆
- □ **crowded** 形混雑した, 満員の

114

WORD LIST

- **cry** 動 泣く, 叫ぶ, 大声を出す, 嘆く cry out 叫ぶ
- **crystal** 名 ①水晶 ②結晶
- **culture** 名 文化
- **cup** 名 カップ, 茶わん
- **curl** 動 カールする
- **curler** 名 (髪を巻く)カーラー
- **curtain** 名 カーテン
- **cut** 動 ①切る, 刈る ②短縮する, 削る ③cutの過去, 過去分詞 cut off 切断する, 切り離す
- **Czechoslovakia** 名 チェコスロバキア《国名》

D

- **daily** 形 毎日の, 日常の
- **dance** 動 踊る, ダンスをする
- **danger** 名 危険, 障害, 脅威 put ~ in danger ~を危険にさらす
- **dangerous** 形 危険な, 有害な
- **dark** 形 ①暗い, 闇の ②(色が)濃い, (髪が)黒い ③陰うつな
- **date** 動 デートする
- **dated** 形 日付のある
- **daughter** 名 娘
- **day** 名 ①日中, 昼間 ②日, 期日 ③《-s》時代, 生涯 every day 毎日 one day (過去の)ある日, (未来の)いつか
- **de Winter** ド・ヴィンテル《人名》
- **dead** 形 死んでいる
- **deal** 動《- with ~》~を扱う
- **death** 名 ①死, 死ぬこと ②《the -》終えん, 消滅 to death 死ぬまで, 死ぬほど
- **December** 名 12月
- **decide** 動 決定[決意]する, (~しようと)決める, 判決を下す decide to do ~することに決める
- **deep** 形 ①深い, 深さ~の ②深遠な ③濃い
- **deliver** 動 配達する
- **dentist** 名 歯医者
- **department store** 名 百貨店
- **depend** 動《- on [upon] ~》①~を頼る, ~をあてにする ②~による
- **describe** 動 (言葉・文章で~を)表現[描写]する
- **desk** 名 机, 台
- **despite** 前 ~にもかかわらず
- **destroy** 動 破壊する, 絶滅させる, 無効にする
- **develop** 動 ①発達する[させる] ②開発する
- **diary** 名 日記
- **did** 動 do (~をする)の過去 助 doの過去
- **die** 動 死ぬ, 消滅する
- **different** 形 異なった, 違った, 別の, さまざまな be different from ~と違う
- **differently** 副 (~と)異なって, 違って
- **difficult** 形 困難な, むずかしい, 扱いにくい
- **dig** 動 ①掘る ②小突く ③探る dig up 掘り起こす, 掘り出す
- **dining room** ダイニングルーム, 食堂
- **dinner** 名 ①ディナー, 夕食 ②夕食[食事]会, 祝宴
- **dirt** 名 土
- **dirty** 形 ①汚い, 汚れた ②卑劣な, 不正な
- **disappear** 動 見えなくなる, 姿を消す, なくなる
- **discover** 動 発見する, 気づく
- **discovery** 名 発見
- **discuss** 動 議論[検討]する
- **disease** 名 病気

- **dish** 名 大皿
- **distant** 形 ①遠い, 隔たった ②よそよそしい, 距離のある
- **do** 助 ①《ほかの動詞とともに用いて現在形の否定文・疑問文をつくる》②《同じ動詞を繰り返す代わりに用いる》③《動詞を強調するのに用いる》動 ～をする **do well** 成績が良い, 成功する
- **doctor** 名 医者, 博士
- **done** 動 do (〜をする)の過去分詞
- **door** 名 ①ドア, 戸 ②一軒, 一戸
- **doorbell** 名 玄関の呼び鈴[ベル]
- **down** 副 ①下へ, 降りて, 低くなって ②倒れて 前 〜の下方へ, 〜を下って 形 下方, 下りの
- **downstairs** 副 階下で, 下の部屋で 形 階下の
- **downtown** 名 街の中心, 繁華街
- **Dr.** 名 〜博士,《医者に対して》〜先生
- **drank** 動 drink (飲む)の過去
- **dream** 名 夢, 幻想
- **dress** 名 ドレス, 衣服, 正装 動 ①服を着る[着せる] ②飾る
- **drinking water** 飲用水
- **duck** 名 カモ, アヒル 動 頭を下げる, 身をかわす
- **during** 前 〜の間(ずっと)
- **Dutch** 形 オランダの 名 オランダ人 **on Dutch soil** オランダ領内で
- **duty** 名 職務, 任務
- **Dwight Eisenhower** ドワイト・アイゼンハワー《米国の軍人, 政治家。第34代大統領。1890-1969》
- **dysentery** 名 赤痢

E

- **each** 形 それぞれの, 各自の **each time** 〜するたびに 代 それぞれ, 各自 **each other** お互いに 副 それぞれに
- **eagerly** 副 熱心に, しきりに
- **early** 形 ①(時間や時期が)早い ②初期の, 幼少の, 若い 副 ①早く, 早めに ②初期に, 初めのころに
- **easy** 形 ①やさしい, 簡単な ②気楽な, くつろいだ
- **eat** 動 食べる, 食事する
- **Edith Frank** エーディト・フランク《アンネの母。1900-1945》
- **Edith Holländer** エーディト・ホーレンダー《エーディト・フランクの旧姓》
- **edition** 名 (本・雑誌などの)版
- **eight** 名 8(の数字), 8人[個] 形 8の, 8人[個]の
- **eighteen** 名 18(の数字), 18人[個] 形 18の, 18人[個]の
- **eighteenth** 名 第18番目(の人[もの]), 18日 形 第18番目の
- **eighth** 名 第8番目(の人[物]), 8日 形 第8番目の
- **Eisenhower** 名 (ドワイト・)アイゼンハワー《米国の軍人, 政治家。第34代大統領。1890-1969》
- **either** 形 ①(2つのうち)どちらかの ②どちらでも 副 ①どちらか ②《否定文で》〜もまた(…ない) 接《〜 or …》〜かまたは…か
- **eleven** 名 ①11(の数字), 11人[個] ②11人のチーム, イレブン 形 11の, 11人[個]の
- **else** 副 ①そのほかに[の], 代わりに ②さもないと **anything else** ほかの何か
- **emergency** 名 非常時, 緊急時 形 緊急の
- **empty** 形 ①空の, 空いている ②(心などが)ぼんやりした, 無意味な
- **encourage** 動 ①勇気づける ②促進する, 助長する
- **end** 名 ①終わり, 終末, 死 ②果て,

Word List

- 末, 端 ③目的 **at the end of** 〜の終わりに **in the end** とうとう, 結局, ついに 動終わる, 終える
- **energy** 名①力, 勢い ②元気, 精力, エネルギー
- **England** 名①イングランド ②英国
- **English** 名①英語 ②《the –》英国人 形①英語の ②英国(人)の
- **enjoyment** 名楽しむこと, 喜び
- **enough** 形十分な, (〜するに)足る **enough to do** 〜するのに十分な 副(〜できる)だけ, 十分に, まったく
- **enter** 動入る
- **entire** 形全体の, 完全な, まったくの
- **entirely** 副完全に, まったく
- **escape** 動逃げる, 免れる, もれる 名逃亡, 脱出, もれ
- **especially** 副特別に, とりわけ
- **Europe** 名ヨーロッパ
- **even** 副①《強意》〜でさえも, 〜ですら, いっそう, なおさら ②平等に **even if** たとえ〜でも
- **evening** 名夕方, 晩
- **ever** 副今までに, これまで, かつて, いつまでも
- **every** 形①どの〜も, すべての, あらゆる ②毎〜, 〜ごとに **every day** 毎日 **every other** 1つおきの〜 **every time** 〜するときはいつも
- **everybody** 代誰でも, 皆
- **everyday** 形毎日の, 日々の
- **everyone** 代誰でも, 皆
- **everything** 代すべてのこと[もの], 何でも, 何もかも
- **everywhere** 副どこにいても, いたるところに
- **evidence** 名①証拠, 証人 ②形跡
- **exactly** 副①正確に, 厳密に, ちょうど ②まったくそのとおり
- **example** 名例, 見本, 模範 **for example** たとえば
- **except** 前〜を除いて, 〜のほかは
- **excited** 形興奮した, わくわくした
- **excitement** 名興奮(すること)
- **exercise** 名運動, 体操
- **exist** 動存在する, 生存する, ある, いる
- **experience** 名経験, 体験 動経験[体験]する
- **experiment** 名実験, 試み
- **explain** 動説明する, 明らかにする, 釈明[弁明]する
- **express** 動表現する, 述べる
- **extra** 形余分の, 臨時の
- **eye** 名目

F

- **face** 名顔, 顔つき
- **factory** 名工場, 製造所
- **fair** 形正しい, 公平[正当]な
- **fairly** 副かなり, 相当に
- **fall** 動①落ちる, 倒れる ②(ある状態に)急に陥る **fall in love** 恋におちる **fall into someone's lap** (人)に(幸運が)舞い込む
- **fallen** 動 fall (落ちる)の過去分詞
- **family** 名家族, 家庭
- **famous** 形有名な, 名高い
- **fantasy** 名空想, 夢想
- **farm** 名農場, 農家
- **fashion** 名①流行, 方法, はやり ②流行のもの(特に服装) **in fashion** 流行して, はやって
- **fast** 形(速度が)速い 副速く, 急いで
- **father** 名父親
- **favorite** 名お気に入り(の人[物])

形 お気に入りの, ひいきの
- **fear** 名 ①恐れ ②心配, 不安 **in fear** おどおどして, ビクビクして **with fear** 怖がって
- **February** 名 2月
- **feel** 動 感じる, (～と)思う **feel like** ～がほしい, ～したい気がする, ～のような感じがする
- **feeling** 名 感じ, 気持ち
- **fell** 動 fall (落ちる)の過去
- **felt** 動 feel (感じる)の過去, 過去分詞
- **female** 形 女性の, 婦人の, 雌の
- **fence** 名 囲み, さく
- **few** 形 ①ほとんどない, 少数の(～しかない) ②《a –》少数の, 少しはある
- **fifteen** 名 15(の数字), 15人[個] 形 15の, 15人[個]の
- **fifth** 名 第5番目(の人[物]), 5日 形 第5番目の
- **fight** 動 (～と)戦う, 争う **fight with** ～と戦う 名 ①戦い, 争い, けんか ②闘志, ファイト
- **fighting** 名 戦闘 **stiff fighting** 過酷な戦い
- **figure** 動 ①描写する, 想像する ②計算する ③目立つ, (～として)現れる **figure out** 考え出す
- **file** 動 とじ込む, 保管する
- **fill** 動 ①満ちる, 満たす ②《be -ed with ～》～でいっぱいである **fill up** (穴・すき間を)いっぱいに満たす, 詰める
- **final** 形 最後の, 決定的な **final solution** 大量殺りく
- **finally** 副 最後に, ついに, 結局
- **find** 動 ①見つける ②(～と)わかる, 気づく, ～と考える ③得る **find out** 見つけ出す, 気がつく, 知る, 調べる, 解明する
- **finish** 動 終わる, 終える

- **fire** 名 ①火, 炎, 火事 ②砲火, 攻撃
- **first** 名 最初, 第一(の人・物) **at first** 最初は, 初めのうちは 形 ①第一の, 最初の ②最も重要な **first floor** 2階《英》 **for the first time** 初めて 副 第一に, 最初に
- **first-person** 形 一人称の, 本人の
- **five** 名 5(の数字), 5人[個] 形 5の, 5人[個]の
- **floor** 名 床, 階 **first floor** 2階 **ground floor** 1階
- **flower** 名 花, 草花
- **follow** 動 ①ついていく, あとをたどる ②(～の)結果として起こる ③(忠告などに)従う
- **food** 名 食物, えさ, 肥料
- **foods industry** 食品産業
- **fool** 動 だます
- **for** 前 ①《目的・原因・対象》～にとって, ～のために[の], ～に対して ②《期間》～間 ③《代理》～の代わりに ④《方向》～へ(向かって) 接 というわけは～, なぜなら～, だから
- **force** 名 力, 勢い 動 ①強制する, 力ずくで～する, 余儀なく～させる ②押しやる, 押し込む
- **forever** 副 永遠に, 絶えず
- **forgave** 動 forgive (許す)の過去
- **fortunately** 副 幸運にも
- **forward** 副 ①前方に ②将来に向けて ③先へ, 進んで **look forward to** ～を期待する
- **fought** 動 fight (戦う)の過去, 過去分詞
- **found** 動 find (見つける)の過去, 過去分詞
- **four** 名 4(の数字), 4人[個] 形 4の, 4人[個]の
- **fourteen** 名 14(の数字), 14人[個] 形 14の, 14人[個]の
- **fourth** 名 第4番目(の人・物), 4日 形 第4番目の

- □ **France** 名 フランス《国名》
- □ **Frank** 名 フランク《人名》
- □ **Frankfurt** 名 フランクフルト《ドイツの都市。フランクフルト・アム・マインの通称》
- □ **Frankfurt-am-Main** フランクフルト・アム・マイン《ドイツの都市》
- □ **free** 形 自由な、開放された、自由に〜できる 動 自由にする、解放する
- □ **freedom** 名 ①自由 ②束縛がないこと
- □ **freely** 副 自由に、障害なしに
- □ **French** 形 フランス(人・語)の 名 ①フランス語 ②《the –》フランス人
- □ **fresh** 形 ①新鮮な、生気のある ②新規の
- □ **Friday** 名 金曜日
- □ **friend** 名 友だち、仲間 make friends with 〜と友達になる
- □ **friendly** 形 親しみのある、親切な、友情のこもった
- □ **friendship** 名 友人であること、友情
- □ **frightened** 形 おびえた、びっくりした
- □ **Fritz Pfeffer** フリッツ・プフェファー《アンネ・フランクらとともに隠れ家に同居していた。ノイエンガンメ強制収容所で死亡。1889-1944》
- □ **from** 前 ①《出身・出発点・時間・順序・原料》〜から ②《原因・理由》〜がもとで from now on 今後
- □ **front** 形 正面の、前面の
- □ **fruit** 名 ①果実、実 ②《-s》成果、利益
- □ **full** 形 ①満ちた、いっぱいの、満期の ②完全な、盛りの、充実した be full of 〜で一杯である full of life 元気いっぱいで、活発な
- □ **fun** 名 楽しみ、冗談、おもしろいこと for fun 楽しみで make fun of 〜を物笑いの種にする、からかう
- □ **funny** 形 ①おもしろい、こっけいな ②奇妙な、うさんくさい
- □ **furniture** 名 家具、備品、調度
- □ **future** 名 未来、将来

G

- □ **game** 名 ゲーム、試合、遊び、競技
- □ **garbage** 名 ごみ、くず
- □ **garden** 名 庭、庭園
- □ **gas** 名 ガス、気体 動 〜を毒ガスで殺す
- □ **gassing** 名 ガス処理
- □ **gather** 動 ①集まる、集める ②生じる、増す ③推測する
- □ **gave** 動 give (与える) の過去
- □ **general** 名 大将、将軍
- □ **German** 形 ドイツ(人・語)の 名 ①ドイツ人 ②ドイツ語
- □ **German-occupied** 形 ドイツ占領下の
- □ **Germany** 名 ドイツ《国名》
- □ **Gestapo** 名 ゲシュタポ《ドイツ警察の秘密警察部門》
- □ **get** 動 ①得る、手に入れる ②(ある状態に)なる、いたる ③わかる、理解する ④〜させる、〜を(…の状態に)する ⑤(ある場所に)達する、着く get into trouble 〜を面倒[トラブル]に巻き込む get away 逃げる、逃亡する、離れる get back 戻る、帰る get in 中に入る、乗り込む get into 〜に入る、入り込む、〜に巻き込まれる get mad 腹を立てる get out of bed 起きる、寝床を離れる get out ①外に出る、出て行く、逃げ出す ②取り出す、抜き出す get ready 用意[支度]をする get someone to do (人)に〜させる[してもらう] get up 起き上がる、立ち上がる get used to 〜になじむ、〜に慣れる get worse 悪化する

- [ ] **gift** 名 ①贈り物 ②(天賦の)才能
- [ ] **girl** 名 女の子, 少女
- [ ] **girlfriend** 名 女友だち
- [ ] **give** 動 ①与える, 贈る ②伝える, 述べる ③(〜を)する
- [ ] **given** 動 give (与える) の過去分詞
- [ ] **glad** 形 ①うれしい, 喜ばしい ②《be – to 〜》〜してうれしい, 喜んで〜する
- [ ] **glass** 名 ガラス(状のもの)
- [ ] **go** 動 ①行く, 出かける ②動く ③進む, 経過する, いたる ④(ある状態に)なる **be going to** 〜するつもりである **go back to** 〜に帰る [戻る], 〜に遡る, (中断していた作業に)再び取り掛かる **go by** ①(時が)過ぎる, 経過する ②〜のそばを通る ③〜に基づいて[よって]行う **go doing** 〜をしに行く **go for** 〜に出かける, 〜を追い求める, 〜を好む **go home** 帰宅する **go into** 〜に入る, (仕事)に就く **go on living** 生きていく **go on** 続く, 続ける, 進み続ける, 起こる, 発生する **go out** 外出する, 外へ出る **go shopping** 買い物に行く **go through** 通り抜ける, 一つずつ順番に検討する **go to sleep** 寝る **go up** ①〜に上がる, 登る ②〜に近づく, 出かける ③(建物などが)建つ, 立つ
- [ ] **goal** 名 目的(地), 目標
- [ ] **god** 名 神
- [ ] **gone** 動 go (行く) の過去分詞 形 去った, 使い果たした, 死んだ
- [ ] **good** 形 ①よい, 上手な, 優れた, 美しい ②(数量・程度が)かなりの, 相当な **be good at** 〜が得意だ
- [ ] **good-looking** 形 顔立ちのよい, ハンサムな, きれいな
- [ ] **goodbye** 名 別れのあいさつ **say goodbye to** 〜にさよならと言う
- [ ] **goods** 名 ①商品, 品物 ②財産, 所有物
- [ ] **Goslar** 名 ホースラル《人名》
- [ ] **got** 動 get (得る) の過去, 過去分詞

- [ ] **government** 名 政府
- [ ] **grade** 名 学年
- [ ] **grandfather** 名 祖父
- [ ] **grandmother** 名 祖母
- [ ] **grandparent** 名 祖父母
- [ ] **grape** 名 ブドウ
- [ ] **grass** 名 草, 牧草(地), 芝生
- [ ] **grateful** 形 感謝する, ありがたく思う
- [ ] **great** 形 ①大きい, 広大な, (量や程度が)たいへんな ②偉大な, 優れた ③すばらしい, おもしろい
- [ ] **grew** 動 grow (成長する) の過去
- [ ] **grey** 形 灰色の 名 灰色
- [ ] **ground** 名 地面, 土, 土地 **ground floor** 1階 **on the ground** 地面に
- [ ] **group** 名 集団, 群
- [ ] **grow** 動 ①成長する, 育つ, 育てる ②増大する, 大きくなる, (次第に〜に)なる **grow up** 成長する, 大人になる
- [ ] **guard** 名 番人
- [ ] **gun** 名 銃
- [ ] **gypsy** 名 ジプシー

H

- [ ] **had** 動 have (持つ) の過去, 過去分詞 助 have の過去《過去完了の文をつくる》
- [ ] **hair** 名 髪, 毛
- [ ] **hairstyle** 名 ヘアスタイル, 髪型
- [ ] **half** 形 半分の, 不完全な
- [ ] **half-hour** 名 半時間, 30分
- [ ] **hand** 名 手 **on the other hand** 一方, 他方では
- [ ] **handsome** 形 端正な(顔立ちの), りっぱな, (男性が)ハンサムな
- [ ] **hang** 動 かかる, かける, つるす, ぶら下がる **hang on** 〜につかまる, し

がみつく, がんばる, (電話を)切らずに待つ
- **Hanneli Goslar** ハンネリ・ホースラル(リース)《アンネの友人で同級生。1928–》
- **Hanukkah** 名 ハヌカ《キリスト教のクリスマスと同時期に祝われるユダヤ教の行事》
- **happen** 動 ①(出来事が)起こる, 生じる ②偶然[たまたま]～する **happen to** たまたま～する, 偶然～する
- **happy** 形 幸せな, うれしい, 幸運な, 満足して **be happy to do** ～してうれしい, 喜んで～する
- **harass** 動 悩ます, 苦しめる, いやがらせる
- **hard** 形 ①堅い ②激しい, むずかしい ③熱心な, 勤勉な ④無情な, 耐えがたい, 厳しい, きつい **a hard time** つらい時期 **hard to** ～し難い 副 ①一生懸命に ②激しく ③堅く
- **has** 動 have (持つ)の3人称単数現在 助 haveの3人称単数現《現在完了の文をつくる》
- **hat** 名 (縁のある)帽子
- **hate** 動 嫌う, 憎む, (～するのを)いやがる
- **hateful** 形 憎らしい, 忌まわしい
- **have** 動 ①持つ, 持っている, 抱く ②(～が)ある, いる ③食べる, 飲む ④経験する, (病気に)かかる ⑤催す, 開く ⑥(人に)～させる **have to** ～しなければならない **have a baby** 赤ちゃんを産む **have a cold** 風邪を引いている **have no choice but to** ～するしかない **have no idea** わからない **have something to say** 言いたいことがある 助《〈have＋過去分詞〉の形で現在完了の文をつくる》～した, ～したことがある, ずっと～している
- **he** 代 彼は[が]
- **head** 名 ①頭 ②先頭 ③長, 指導者 **head of** ～の長 動 向かう, 向ける

- **health** 名 健康(状態), 衛生, 保健
- **healthy** 形 健康な, 健全な, 健康によい
- **hear** 動 聞く, 聞こえる **hear about** ～について聞く **hear from** ～から手紙[電話・返事]をもらう
- **heard** 動 hear (聞く)の過去, 過去分詞
- **heart** 名 ①心臓, 胸 ②心, 感情, ハート ③中心, 本質 **at heart** 心底では, 実際は
- **heartbroken** 形 悲しみに打ちひしがれた
- **heavily** 副 ①重く, 重そうに, ひどく ②多量に
- **Hebrew** 名 ヘブライ語
- **height** 名 ①高さ, 身長 ②《the –》絶頂, 真っ盛り ③高台, 丘
- **Hello Silberberg** ヘルムート・(ヘロー・)シルベルベルフ《Helmuth –, アンネのボーイフレンド》
- **help** 動 ①助ける, 手伝う ②給仕する **help in** ～に役立つ **help ～ with** ……を～の面で手伝う
- **helper** 名 助手, 助けになるもの
- **helpful** 形 役に立つ, 参考になる
- **her** 代 ①彼女を[に] ②彼女の
- **Herbert** 名 ヘルベルト《オットーの兄》
- **here** 副 ここに[で]
- **Hermann van Pels** ヘルマン・ファン・ペルス《アンネ・フランクらとともに隠れ家に同居していた。アウシュヴィッツ＝ビルケナウ強制収容所でガス車送りとなり死亡。1898–1944》
- **herself** 代 彼女自身
- **hid** 動 hide (隠れる)の過去, 過去分詞
- **hidden** 動 hide (隠れる)の過去分詞 形 隠れた, 秘密の
- **hide** 動 隠れる, 隠れて見えない, 秘密にする

THE STORY OF ANNE FRANK

- **hiding** 名隠れ場所
- **high school** 高校
- **him** 代彼を[に]
- **himself** 代彼自身
- **hint** 動暗示する, ほのめかす
- **hire** 動雇う, 賃借りする
- **his** 代①彼の ②彼のもの
- **history** 名歴史, 経歴
- **Hitler** 名(アドルフ・)ヒトラー《Adolf –, ドイツの政治家, 1889–1945》
- **hold** 動つかむ, 持つ, 抱く
- **holiday** 名祝祭日, 休暇
- **Holland** 名オランダ《国》
- **Hollywood** 名ハリウッド《アメリカの地名》
- **Holocaust** 名ホロコースト《「大虐殺・大惨害」を意味するが, とくにナチスによるユダヤ人大虐殺を指す》
- **holy** 形聖なる, 神聖な
- **home** 名①家, 自国, 故郷, 家庭 ②収容所 **at home** 在宅して **bring home** 家に持ってくる **go home** 帰宅する
- **homosexual** 名同性愛(者)
- **honest** 形①正直な, 誠実な, 心からの ②公正な, 感心な
- **hope** 名希望, 期待, 見込み 動望む, (~であるようにと)思う
- **horrific** 形恐ろしい
- **horror** 名①恐怖, ぞっとすること ②嫌悪
- **hospital** 名病院
- **hot bath** (高)温浴
- **hotel** 名ホテル, 旅館
- **hour** 名1時間, 時間
- **house** 名家, 家庭
- **household** 形家庭(用)の
- **housekeeper** 名家政婦
- **how** 副①どうやって, どれくらい, どんなふうに ②なんて(~だろう) ③《関係副詞》~する方法 **How about ~ ?** ~はどうですか。~しませんか。 **how to** ~する方法
- **however** 接けれども, だが
- **huge** 形巨大な, ばく大な
- **human** 形人間の, 人の 名人間
- **humanity** 名人間性, 人間らしさ
- **hundred** 名①100(の数字), 100人[個] ②《-s》何百, 多数 **hundreds of** 何百もの~ 形①100の, 100人[個]の ②多数の
- **hunger** 名空腹, 飢え
- **hurry** 名急ぐこと, 急ぐ必要 **in a hurry** 急いで, あわてて
- **hurt** 動傷つける, 痛む, 害する 名傷, けが, 苦痛, 害
- **husband** 名夫

I

- **I** 代私は[が]
- **ice skate** アイス・スケートをする
- **idea** 名考え, 意見, アイデア, 計画 **have no idea** わからない
- **ideal** 名理想, 究極の目標
- **if** 接もし~ならば, たとえ~でも, ~かどうか **as if** あたかも~のように, まるで~みたいに **even if** たとえ~でも **what if** もし~だったらどうなるだろうか
- **illness** 名病気
- **important** 形重要な, 大切な, 有力な
- **impossible** 形不可能な, できない, あり[起こり]えない
- **improve** 動改善する[させる], 進歩する
- **in** 前①《場所・位置・所属》~(の中)に[で・の] ②《時》~(の時)に[の・で], ~後(に), ~の間(に) ③《方法・手段》~で ④~を身につけて, ~を着て ⑤

WORD LIST

- □ ～に関して，～について ⑥《状態》～の状態で 中へ[に], 内へ[に]
- □ **include** 動 含む，勘定に入れる
- □ **incredible** 形 ①信じられない，信用できない ②すばらしい，とてつもない
- □ **independent** 形 独立した，自立した
- □ **individual** 形 独立した，個性的な，個々の
- □ **industry** 名 産業，工業
- □ **infect** 動 ①感染する，伝染する ②（病気を）移す ③影響を及ぼす
- □ **information** 名 ①情報，通知，知識 ②案内（所），受付（係）
- □ **inside** 形 内部[内側]にある 副 内部[内側]に 前 ～の内部[内側]に
- □ **instead** 副 その代わりに
- □ **instrument** 名 ①道具，器具，器械 ②楽器
- □ **interested** 形 興味を持った，関心のある be interested in ～に興味[関心]がある
- □ **into** 前 ①《動作・運動の方向》～の中へ[に] ②《変化》～に[へ]
- □ **introduction** 名 紹介，導入
- □ **invite** 動 ①招待する，招く ②勧める，誘う ③～をもたらす
- □ **Iowa** 名 アイオワ《アメリカの州》
- □ **is** 動 be（～である）の3人称単数現在
- □ **it** 代 ①それは[が], それを[に] ②《天候・日時・距離・寒暖などを示す》It is ～ for someone to … （人）が …するのは～だ
- □ **its** 代 それの，あれの

J

- □ **jacket** 名 短い上着
- □ **Jacqueline van Maarsen** ジャクリーヌ・ファン・マールセン《アンネのユダヤ人中学校での友達。1929-》
- □ **Jan Gies** ヤン・ヒース《オランダのレジスタンス活動家，アンネたちの隠れ家での生活を支援したミープ・ヒースの夫。1905-1993》
- □ **Janny Brilleslijper** ヤニ・ブリレスレイベル《ヴェステルボルク収容所でアンネたちと知り合う。ベルゲン・ベルゼン収容所で再会する。1918-2003》
- □ **January** 名 1月
- □ **Japan** 名 日本《国名》
- □ **Jew** 名 ユダヤ人，ユダヤ教徒
- □ **jewelry** 名 宝石，宝飾品類
- □ **Jewish** 形 ユダヤ人の，ユダヤ教の
- □ **Jewish-owned** 形 ユダヤ人の所有する
- □ **job** 名 仕事，職，雇用
- □ **Johannes Kleiman** ヨハネス・クレイマン《会計士。後でオットーの会社の所有者となり，フランク一家をサポートする。1896-1959》
- □ **join** 動 一緒になる，参加する
- □ **joke** 名 冗談，ジョーク
- □ **Joseph Mengele** ヨーゼフ・メンゲレ《ナチスの医師，親衛隊の将校。人体実験のためのユダヤ人の選別を行い，「死の天使」と恐れられた。1911-1979》
- □ **journalist** 名 報道関係者，ジャーナリスト
- □ **joy** 名 喜び，楽しみ
- □ **Juanita Wagner** ホワニータ・ワーグナー《アンネの文通友達》
- □ **Judy de Winter** ユーディー・ド・ヴィンテル《アンネと収容所で知り合う友達になる》
- □ **juice** 名 ジュース，液，汁
- □ **Julius** 名 ユリウス《エーディトの兄》
- □ **July** 名 7月

- ☐ **jump** 動 ①跳ぶ, 躍進する, 飛び越える, 飛びかかる ②(〜を)熱心にやり始める **jump into** 〜に飛び込む
- ☐ **June** 名 6月
- ☐ **just** 副 ①まさに, ちょうど, (〜した)ばかり ②ほんの, 単に, ただ〜だけ ③ちょっと **just as** (ちょうど)であろうとおり **just then** そのとたんに

K

- ☐ **Kamp Westerbork** ヴェステルボルク通過収容所《強制収容所に移送されるまでの一時収容所》
- ☐ **Kathi** 名 キャシー《フランク家のお手伝いさん》
- ☐ **keep** 動 ①とっておく, 保つ, 続ける ②(〜を…に)しておく ③飼う, 養う ④経営する ⑤守る **keep someone from** (人)に〜させない(ようにする) **keep up** 続ける, 続く, 維持する, (遅れないで)ついていく, 上げたままにしておく
- ☐ **Keesing** 名 キーシング《アンネの学校の先生》
- ☐ **kept** 動 keep (とっておく)の過去, 過去分詞
- ☐ **kill** 動 殺す, 消す, 枯らす
- ☐ **killing** 名 殺害, 殺人
- ☐ **kind** 形 親切な, 優しい 名 種類 **kind of** ある程度, いくらか, 〜のような物[人]
- ☐ **kindergarten** 名 幼稚園
- ☐ **kiss** 動 キスする
- ☐ **kitchen** 名 台所, 調理場
- ☐ **Kitty** 名 キティー《アンネが日記帳につけた名前》
- ☐ **knew** 動 know (知っている)の過去
- ☐ **know** 動 ①知っている, 知る, (〜が)わかる, 理解している ②知り合いである
- ☐ **known** 動 know (知っている)の過去分詞 **be known as** 〜として知られている **be known to** 〜に知られている
- ☐ **Kristallnacht** 名 水晶の夜/クリスタルナハト《1938年11月9日の夜から10日未明にかけ, ドイツ全土で行われたナチスによるユダヤ人の迫害. 割れたガラス窓の破片がキラキラ光っていたことから名付けられた》
- ☐ **Kuperus** クペルス《アンネの学校の先生》

L

- ☐ **lady** 名 婦人, 夫人, 淑女, 奥さん
- ☐ **language** 名 言語, 言葉, 国語, 〜語, 専門語
- ☐ **lap** 名 ひざ **fall into someone's lap** (人)に(幸運が)舞い込む
- ☐ **large** 形 ①大きい, 広い ②大勢の, 多量の
- ☐ **last** 形 ①《the -》最後の ②この前の, 先〜 ③最新の **the last time** この前〜したとき 動 続く, 持ちこたえる
- ☐ **lately** 副 近ごろ, 最近
- ☐ **later** 副 後で, 後ほど
- ☐ **laugh** 動 笑う 名 笑い(声) **make someone laugh** (人)を笑わせる
- ☐ **laughter** 名 笑い(声)
- ☐ **law** 名 法, 法律
- ☐ **lay** 動 lie (横たわる)の過去
- ☐ **lead** 動 ①導く, 案内する ②(生活を)送る **lead into** (ある場所)へ導く **lead to** 〜に至る, 〜に通じる, 〜を引き起こす
- ☐ **leader** 名 指導者, リーダー
- ☐ **learn** 動 学ぶ, 習う, 教わる, 知識[経験]を得る
- ☐ **leave** 動 ①出発する, 去る ②残す, 置き忘れる ③(〜を…の)ままにし

- ておく ④ゆだねる **leave for** ~に向かって出発する
- □ **led** 動 lead（導く）の過去, 過去分詞
- □ **lees** リース《Lies（アンネの友人ハンネリ・ホースラルの愛称）のリスペリング（綴り替え）》
- □ **left** 動 leave（去る, ~をあとに残す）の過去, 過去分詞
- □ **Leni** 名 レニ《オットーの妹》
- □ **less** 形 ~より少なく, ~ほどでなく
- □ **lesson** 名 授業, 学科, 課, けいこ
- □ **let** 動（人に~）させる,（~するのを）許す,（~をある状態に）する
- □ **letter** 名 手紙
- □ **lettuce** 名 レタス
- □ **library** 名 図書館
- □ **lie** 動 ①うそをつく ②横たわる, 寝る ③（ある状態に）ある, 存在する
- **Lientje Brilleslijper** リーンチェ・ブリレスレイベル《ヴェステルボルク収容所でアンネたちと知り合う。ベルゲン・ベルゼン収容所で再会する》
- □ **Lies** リース《アンネの友人で同級生ハンネリ・ホースラルの愛称》
- □ **life** 名 ①生命, 生物 ②一生, 生涯, 人生 ③生活, 暮らし, 世の中 **all one's life** ずっと, 生まれてから **come to life** 目覚める, 復活する **full of life** 元気いっぱいで, 活発な **way of life** 生き様, 生き方, 暮らし方
- □ **like** 動 好む, 好きである 前 ~に似ている, ~のような **feel like** ~がほしい, ~したい気がする, ~のような感じがする **like this** このような, こんなふうに **look like** ~のように見える, ~に似ている **sound like** ~のように聞こえる 形 似ている, ~のような
- □ **line** 名 列 **in line** 一列に 動 整列する
- □ **list** 名 名簿, 目録, 一覧表 動 名簿[目録]に記入する
- □ **listen** 動《- to ~》~を聞く, ~に耳を傾ける
- □ **little** 形 ①小さい, 幼い ②少しの, 短い ③ほとんど~ない,《a -》少しはある 名 少し（しか）, 少量 **little by little** 少しずつ 副 全然~ない,《a -》少しはある
- □ **live** 動 住む, 暮らす, 生きている **go on living** 生きていく **live on** ~を糧として生きる **live through**（危機などを）乗り越える
- □ **lively** 形 ①元気のよい, 活発な ②鮮やかな, 強烈な, 真に迫った
- □ **lives** life（生命）の複数
- □ **living** 動 live（住む）の現在分詞 名 生計, 生活
- □ **living room** 居間
- □ **lock** 錠をドろす, 閉じ込める, 動けなくする
- □ **long** 形 ①長い, 長期の ②《長さ・距離・時間などを示す語句を伴って》~の長さ[距離・時間]の 副 長い間, ずっと **as long as** ~する以上は, ~である限りは **no longer** もはや~でない[~しない] 名 長い期間 **for long** 長い間 **take long** 時間がかかる 動 切望する, 思い焦がれる
- □ **look** 動 ①見る ②（~に）見える,（~の）顔つきをする ③注意する ④《間投詞のように》ほら, ねえ **look for** ~を探す **look forward to** ~を期待する **look like** ~のように見える, ~に似ている **look out** ①外を見る ②気をつける, 注意する **look through** ~をのぞき込む **look up** 見上げる, 調べる
- □ **looking** 形 ~に見える
- □ **lose** 動 ①失う, 迷う, 忘れる ②負ける, 失敗する
- □ **lost** 動 lose（失う）の過去, 過去分詞
- □ **lot** 名 ①くじ, 運 ②地所, 区画 ③たくさん, たいへん,《a - of ~ / -s of ~》たくさんの~ ④やつ, 連中
- □ **loud** 形 大声の, 騒がしい 副 大声

に[で]
- **love** 名 愛, 愛情, 思いやり be in love with ～に恋して, ～に心を奪われて fall in love 恋におちる 動 愛する, 恋する, 大好きである
- **luck** 名 運, 幸運, めぐり合わせ
- **lucky** 形 幸運な, 運のよい, 縁起のよい lucky for (人)にとってラッキーだったことには
- **lunch** 名 昼食, ランチ, 軽食
- **lying** 動 lie (横たわる)の現在分詞

M

- **Macy's** 名 メーシーズ《アメリカの百貨店》
- **mad** 形 逆上した, 理性をなくした get mad 腹を立てる
- **made** 動 make (作る)の過去, 過去分詞 be made to ～させられる
- **mail** 名 郵便, メール
- **mail opening** 名 (扉の)郵便受け口
- **mailman** 名 郵便配達人
- **major** 形 主な
- **make** 動 ①作る, 得る ②行う, (～に)なる ③(～を…に)する, (～を…)させる make ～ out of … ～を…から作る make a mistake 間違いをする make friends with ～と友達になる make fun of ～を物笑いの種にする, からかう make into ～を…に仕立てる make it to ～にたどり着く make noise 音を立てる make out 作り上げる, 認識する, 見分ける make progress 進歩[上達]する, 前進する make sense 意味をなす, よくわかる make someone laugh (人)を笑わせる make sure 確かめる, 確認する
- **male** 名 男, 雄
- **man** 名 男性, 人, 人類
- **manage** 動 どうにか～する
- **manner** 名《-s》行儀, 作法, 生活様式
- **many** 形 多数の, たくさんの so many 非常に多くの
- **march** 名《M-》3月 動 行進する[させる]
- **Margot Betti Frank** マルゴット・ベッティ・フランク《アンネの姉, ベルゲン・ベルゼン強制収容所で死亡。1926–1945》
- **mark** 名 印, 記号, 跡
- **married** 動 marry (結婚する)の過去, 過去分詞 形 結婚した, 既婚の
- **mass** 名 多数, 多量
- **math** 名 数学
- **matter** 名 物, 事, 事件, 問題 a matter of ～の問題 not matter 問題にならない
- **may** 動 ①～かもしれない ②～してもよい, ～できる 名《M-》5月
- **me** 代 私を[に]
- **mean** 動 意味する 形 卑怯な, けちな, 意地悪な
- **meant** 動 mean (意味する)の過去, 過去分詞
- **measure** 動 測る, (～の)寸法がある
- **meat** 名 肉
- **medical** 形 医学の
- **meet** 動 ①会う, 知り合いになる ②合流する, 交わる ③(条件などに)達する, 合う
- **meeting** 名 集まり, ミーティング set up a meeting ミーティングを設定する
- **member** 名 一員, メンバー
- **men** 名 man (男性)の複数
- **mental** 形 ①心の, 精神の ②知能[知性]の
- **Merwedeplein** 名 メルウェーデプレイン《アムステルダムの地名》
- **message** 名 伝言, (作品などに込

Word List

- められた)メッセージ
- **met** 動 meet(会う)の過去, 過去分詞
- **Miep Gies** ミープ・ヒース《アンネ・フランクらの隠れ家での生活を支援していたオーストリア系オランダ人女性。1909–2010》
- **Miep Santrouschitz** ミープ・ザントロシェッツ《ミープ・ヒースの旧姓》
- **might** 動《may の過去》①～かもしれない ②～してもよい, ～できる
- **mile** 名 マイル《長さの単位。1,609m》
- **milk** 名 牛乳, ミルク
- **million** 名 ①100万 ②《-s》数百万, 多数 形 ①100万の ②多数の
- **Milly** 名 ミリー《オットーのいとこ》
- **mind** 名 ①心, 精神, 考え ②知性
- **minute** 名 ①(時間の)分 ②ちょっとの間
- **miss** 動 (～が)ないのに気づく, (人が)いなくてさびしく思う
- **missing** 形 ①欠けている, 行方不明の ②《the –》行方不明者
- **mistake** 名 誤り, 誤解, 間違い by mistake 誤って make a mistake 間違いをする
- **moment** 名 ①瞬間, ちょっとの間 ②(特定の)時, 時期 at the moment 今は
- **Monday** 名 月曜日
- **money** 名 金, 通貨
- **money-hungry** 形 金に飢えた
- **Montessori** 名 モンテッソーリ(教育)《20世紀始めにマリア・モンテッソーリによって考案された教育法》
- **month** 名 月, 1カ月
- **Moortje** 名 モールチェ《アンネの飼っていた猫の名前》
- **more** 形 ①もっと多くの ②それ以上の, 余分の 副 もっと, さらに多く, いっそう more and more ますます more than ～以上
- **morning** 名 朝, 午前
- **most** 形 ①最も多い ②たいていの, 大部分の 代 ①大部分, ほとんど ②最多数, 最大限 most of all とりわけ, 中でも 副 最も(多く)
- **mother** 名 母, 母親
- **move** 動 ①動く, 動かす ②感動させる ③引っ越す, 移動する be moved 感激する, 感銘する move around あちこち移動する move in 引っ越す move to ～に引っ越す
- **movie** 名 映画, 映画館
- **Mr.** 名《男性に対して》～さん, ～氏, ～先生
- **Mrs.** 名《結婚している女性に対して》～さん, ～夫人, ～先生
- **much** 形 (量・程度が)多くの, 多量の 副 ①とても, たいへん ②《比較級・最上級を修飾して》ずっと, はるかに as much as ～と同じだけ 名 多量, たくさん, 重要なもの too much 過度の
- **murder** 動 殺す
- **musical instrument** 楽器
- **my** 代 私の
- **myself** 代 私自身

N

- **naked** 形 ①裸の, むき出しの ②覆いのない, ありのままの
- **name** 名 ①名前 ②名声 ③《-s》悪口 動 ①名前をつける ②名指しする
- **narrow** 形 狭い
- **nation** 名 国, 国家
- **natural** 形 ①自然の, 天然の ②生まれつきの, 天性の ③当然な
- **Nazi** 名 ナチ, ナチス, 国家社会党(員)
- **Nazi-occupied** 形 ナチス占領下

- **near** 前 ~の近くに, ~のそばに
- **neat** 形 きちんとした, きれいな
- **need** 動 (~を)必要とする, 必要である **need to do** ~する必要がある 名 《-s》必要なもの
- **neighbor** 名 隣人, 隣り合うもの
- **neighborhood** 名 近所(の人々), 付近
- **neither** 形 どちらの~も…でない 代 (2者のうち)どちらも~でない 副 《否定文に続いて》~も…しない **neither ~ nor …** ~も…もない
- **nephew** 名 おい(甥)
- **Neuengamme** 名 ノイエンガンメ強制収容所
- **never** 副 決して[少しも]~ない, 一度も[二度と]~ない
- **new** 形 ①新しい, 新規の ②新鮮な, できたての
- **New York** ニューヨーク《米国の都市;州》
- **newly** 副 再び, 最近, 新たに
- **news** 名 報道, ニュース, 便り, 知らせ
- **newspaper** 名 新聞(紙)
- **next** 形 ①次の, 翌~ ②隣の **next to** ~のとなりに, ~の次に 副 ①次に ②隣に
- **nice** 形 すてきな, よい, きれいな, 親切な
- **niece** 名 めい(姪)
- **night** 名 夜, 晩
- **nine** 名 9(の数字), 9人[個] 形 9の, 9人[個]の
- **no** 副 ①いいえ, いや ②少しも~ない **no longer** もはや~でない[~しない] 形 ~がない, 少しも~ない, ~どころでない, ~禁止 名 否定, 拒否
- **no one** 代 誰も[一人も]~ない
- **nobody** 代 誰も[1人も]~ない
- **noise** 名 騒音, 騒ぎ, 物音 **make noise** 音を立てる
- **none** 代 (~の)何も[誰も・少しも]…ない
- **nor** 接 ~もまたない **neither ~ nor …** ~も…もない
- **normal** 形 普通の, 平均の, 標準的な
- **north** 名 《the -》北, 北部 形 北の, 北からの
- **not** 副 ~でない, ~しない **not always** 必ずしも~であるとは限らない **not matter** 問題にならない **not yet** まだ~してない
- **note** 名 メモ, 覚え書き
- **nothing** 代 何も~ない[しない]
- **notice** 動 ①気づく, 認める ②通告する
- **November** 名 11月
- **now** 副 ①今(では), 現在 ②今すぐ ③では, さて 名 今, 現在 **from now on** 今後 形 今の, 現在の
- **number** 名 ①数, 数字, 番号 ②~号, ~番 《-s》多数
- **nurse** 名 ①看護師[人] ②乳母

O

- **o'clock** 副 ~時
- **occupy** 動 占領する, 保有する
- **October** 名 10月
- **of** 前 ①《所有・所属・部分》~の, ~に属する ②《性質・特徴・材料》~の, ~製の ③《部分》~のうち ④《分離・除去》~から **of course** もちろん, 当然
- **off** 副 ①離れて ②はずれて ③止まって ④休んで
- **office** 名 ①会社, 事務所, 職場, 役所, 局 ②官職, 地位, 役
- **officer** 名 役人, 公務員, 警察官
- **official** 形 公式の, 正式の

Word List

- **officially** 副 公式に, 職務上, 正式に
- **often** 副 しばしば, たびたび
- **oh** 間 ああ, おや, まあ
- **oil** 名 油, 石油
- **old** 形 ①年取った, 老いた ②〜歳の ③古い, 昔の 名 昔, 老人
- **Oma** 名 オマ《アンネの母方の祖母の呼び名》
- **Omi** 名 オミ《アンネの父方の祖母の呼び名》
- **on** 前 ①《場所・接触》〜(の上)に ②《日・時》〜に, 〜と同時に, 〜のすぐ後で ③《関係・従事》〜に関して, 〜について, 〜して 副 〜を身につけて, 上に ②前へ, 続けて **on and on** 延々と, 長々と, 引き続き
- **once** 副 ①一度, 1回 ②かつて **once and for all** これを最後にきっぱりと 接 いったん〜すると
- **one** 名 1 (の数字), 1人[個] one by one 1つずつ, 1人ずつ 形 ①1の, 1人[個] の ②ある 〜 ③《the 〜》唯一の **one day**(過去の)ある日, (未来の)いつか **one side** 片側 代 ①(一般の)人, ある物 ②一方, 片方 ③〜なもの **one of** 〜の1つ[人] **this one** これ, こちら
- **oneself** 熟 **for oneself** 独力で, 自分のために
- **only** 形 唯一の 副 ①単に, 〜にすぎない, ただ〜だけ ②やっと
- **onto** 前 〜の上へ[に]
- **Opekta** 名 オペクタ商会《社名》
- **open** 動 ①開く, 始まる ②広がる, 広げる ③打ち明ける **open up** 心を打ち明ける, 打ち解ける
- **opening** 名 開いた所, 穴 **mail opening** (扉の)郵便受け口
- **opinion** 名 意見, 見識, 世論, 評判
- **opportunity** 名 好機, 適当な時期[状況]
- **or** 接 ①〜か…, または ②さもないと ③すなわち, 言い換えると
- **order** 名 ①順序 ②整理, 整頓 ③命令, 注文(品) 動 ①(〜するよう)命じる, 注文する ②整頓する, 整理する
- **organize** 動 組織する
- **other** 形 ①ほかの, 異なった ②(2つのうち)もう一方の, (3つ以上のうち)残りの **every other** 1つおきの 〜 **on the other hand** 一方, 他方では 代 ①ほかの人[物] ②《the 〜》残りの1つ **each other** お互いに 副 そうでなく, 別に
- **Otto Frank** オットー・フランク《アンネの父, 家族でただ一人, 戦後生き残る。1889–1980》
- **our** 代 私たちの
- **out** 副 ①外へ[に], 不在で, 離れて ②世に出て ③消えて ④すっかり **go out** 外出する, 外へ出る **make 〜 out of ...** 〜を…から作る **make out** 作り上げる, 認識する, 見分ける **out of** ①〜から外へ, 〜から抜け出して ②〜から作り出して, 〜を材料として ③〜の範囲外に, 〜から離れて ④(ある数)の中から 形 ①外の, 遠く離れた ②公表された 前 〜から外へ[に] 動 ①追い出す ②露見する ③(スポーツで)アウトにする
- **outside** 名 外部, 外側 形 外部の, 外側の 副 外へ, 外側に 前 〜の外に[で・の・へ], 〜の範囲を越えて
- **over** 前 ①〜の上に[に], 〜を一面に覆って ②〜を越えて, 〜以上に, 〜よりまさって ③〜の向こう側の[に] ④〜の間 **all over the world** 世界中に **all over** 〜中で, 全体に亘って, 〜の至る所で, 全て終わって, もうだめで 副 上に, 一面に, ずっと **be over** 終わる **take over** 引き継ぐ, 支配する, 乗っ取る 形 ①上部の, 上位の, 過多の ②終わって, すんで
- **own** 形 自身の **of one's own** 自分自身の 動 持っている, 所有する
- **owner** 名 持ち主, オーナー

THE STORY OF ANNE FRANK

P

- **pack** 動 荷造りする, 詰め込む
- **page** 名 ページ
- **pain** 名 痛み
- **pair** 名 (2つから成る)一対, 一組, ペア
- **pal** 友人, 友だち pen pal ペンフレンド
- **paper** 名 ①紙 ②新聞, 論文, 答案 ③《-s》書類
- **parent** 名 ①《-s》両親 ②先祖
- **park** 名 公園, 広場
- **part** 名 ①部分, 割合 ②役目
- **party** 名 ①パーティー, 会, 集まり ②政党, 党
- **pass** 動 ①過ぎる, 通る ②(年月が)たつ pass down (次の世代に)伝える
- **Passover** 名 過越の祭り《ユダヤ人の三大祝節の一つ》
- **past** 形 過去の, この前の 副 通り越して, 過ぎて walk past 通り過ぎる
- **patient** 名 病人, 患者
- **pattern** 名 柄, 型, 模様
- **pay** 動 支払う, 払う, 報いる
- **peace** 名 ①平和 ②平穏
- **Pectacon** 名 ペクタコン商会《社名》
- **pen** 名 ペン pen pal ペンフレンド
- **pencil** 名 鉛筆
- **people** 名 ①(一般に)人々 ②民衆, 世界の人々, 国民, 民族 ③人間
- **perfect** 形 ①完璧な, 完全な ②純然たる
- **person** 名 ①人 ②人格, 人柄
- **personal** 形 ①個人の, 私的な ②本人自らの
- **Peter Schiff** ペーテル・スヒフ《アンネの最初のボーイフレンド》
- **Peter van Pels** ペーター・ファン・ペルス《アンネと同じ年の少年。隠れ家生活をともにし, アンネとも仲良くなる。マウトハウゼン強制収容所で死亡》
- **Pfeffer** 名 (フリッツ・)プフェファー《アンネ・フランクらとともに隠れ家に同居していた。ノイエンガンメ強制収容所で死亡。1889–1944》
- **photo** 名 写真
- **photograph** 名 写真
- **physical** 形 ①物質の, 物理学の, 自然科学の ②身体の, 肉体の
- **pick** 動 ①(花・果実などを)摘む, もぐ ②選ぶ, 精選する ③つつく, ついて穴をあける, ほじくり出す ④(~を)摘み取る be picked on いじめられる
- **picture** 名 絵, 写真 take a picture 写真を撮る
- **pie** 名 パイ
- **piece** 名 ①一片, 部分 ②1個, 1本
- **pile** 名 積み重ね, (~の)山
- **place** 名 ①場所, 建物 ②余地, 空間 ③《one's -》家, 部屋 take place 行われる, 起こる 動 ①置く, 配置する ②任命する, 任じる
- **plan** 名 計画, 設計(図), 案 動 計画する plan to do ~するつもりである
- **play** 動 ①遊ぶ, 競技する ②(楽器を)演奏する, (役を)演じる play with ~で遊ぶ, ~と一緒に遊ぶ 名 遊び, 競技, 劇
- **pleasant** 形 ①(物事が)楽しい, 心地よい ②快活な, 愛想のよい
- **p.m.** 午後
- **pocket** 名 ①ポケット, 袋 ②所持金
- **poem** 名 詩
- **poetry** 名 詩歌, 詩を書くこと
- **point** 名 ①先, 先端 ②点 ③地点, 時点, 箇所 ④《the -》要点 動 (~を)

Word List

- 指す, 向ける
- **poison** 名 毒, 毒薬
- **Poland** 名 ポーランド《国名》
- **police** 名 警察, 警官
- **Polish** 形 ポーランド(人)の
- **polite** 形 ていねいな, 礼儀正しい, 洗練された
- **political** 形 ①政治の, 政党の ②策略的な
- **pool** 名 プール
- **poor** 形 貧しい, 乏しい, 粗末な, 貧弱な
- **poorly** 副 ①貧しく, 乏しく ②へたに
- **popular** 形 ①人気のある, 流行の ②一般的な, 一般向きの
- **possible** 形 ①可能な ②ありうる, 起こりうる as 〜 as possible できるだけ〜
- **possibly** 副 ①あるいは, たぶん ②《否定文, 疑問文で》どうしても, できる限り, とても, なんとか
- **potato** 名 ジャガイモ
- **pouring** 形 土砂降りの
- **power** 名 力, 能力, 才能, 勢力, 権力
- **powerful** 形 力強い, 実力のある, 影響力のある
- **practice** 動 実行する, 練習[訓練]する
- **pray** 動 祈る, 懇願する
- **prayer** 名 ①祈り, 祈願(文) ②祈る人
- **precious** 形 ①貴重な, 高価な ②かわいい, 大事な
- **preference** 名 好きであること, 好み
- **prepare** 動 ①準備[用意]をする ②覚悟する[させる] prepare for 〜 の準備をする
- **present** 名 贈り物, プレゼント
- **press** 動 圧する, 押す
- **pretty** 形 ①かわいい, きれいな ②相当の 副 かなり, 相当, 非常に
- **price** 名 ①値段, 代価, 代償, 犠牲 ②《-s》物価, 相場
- **princess** 名 王女
- **Prinsengracht** 名 プリンセンフラハト通り《アムステルダムの地名》
- **prison** 名 ①刑務所, 監獄 ②監禁
- **prisoner** 名 囚人, 捕虜
- **privacy** 名 (干渉されない)自由な生活, プライバシー
- **private** 形 ①私的な, 個人の ②民間の, 私立の ③内密の, 人里離れた
- **probably** 副 たぶん, あるいは
- **problem** 名 問題, 難問
- **progress** 名 ①進歩, 前進 ②成り行き, 経過 make progress 進歩[上達]する, 前進する
- **promise** 動 約束する
- **proper** 形 ①適した, 適切な, 正しい ②固有の
- **proud** 形 ①自慢の, 誇った, 自尊心のある ②高慢な, 尊大な be proud of 〜 を自慢に思う
- **public** 形 公の, 公開の
- **publicly** 副 公に, 公然と, 人前で, 世間に
- **publish** 動 ①発表[公表]する ②出版[発行]する
- **publisher** 名 出版社, 発行者
- **pure** 形 ①純粋な, 混じりけのない ②罪のない, 清い
- **put** 動 ①置く, のせる ②入れる, つける ③(ある状態に)する ④put の過去, 過去分詞 put 〜 into … 〜を…の状態にする, 〜を…に突っ込む put 〜 in danger 〜を危険にさらす put aside わきに置く put in 〜の中に入れる put on 〜を催す, 上演する
- **puzzle** 名 パズル

Q

- **quack** 動 (アヒルなどが) ガーガー鳴く
- **question** 名 質問, 疑問, 問題
- **quickly** 副 敏速に, 急いで
- **quiet** 形 ①静かな, 穏やかな, じっとした ②おとなしい, 無口な, 目立たない 動 静まる, 静める

R

- **radio** 名 ラジオ
- **raid** 名 急襲 air raid 空襲
- **rain** 名 雨, 降雨
- **raincoat** 名 レインコート
- **rainy** 形 雨降りの, 雨の多い
- **raise** 動 上げる, 高める
- **ran** 動 run (走る) の過去
- **rang** 動 ring (鳴る) の過去
- **rapidly** 副 速く, 急速, すばやく, 迅速に
- **rather** 副 ①むしろ, かえって ②かなり, いくぶん, やや ③それどころか逆に rather than ~よりむしろ
- **reach** 動 着く, 到着する
- **read** 動 読む, 読書する read out 声を出して読む, 読み上げる
- **reading** 動 read (読む) の現在分詞 名 読書, 読み物, 朗読
- **ready** 形 用意 [準備] ができた, まさに~しようとする, 今にも~せんばかりの be ready for 準備が整って, ~に期待する be ready to すぐに [いつでも] ~できる, ~する構えで get ready 用意 [支度] をする 動 用意 [準備] する
- **real** 形 実際の, 実在する, 本物の
- **realize** 動 理解する, 実現する
- **really** 副 本当に, 実際に, 確かに
- **reason** 名 理由
- **receive** 動 ①受け取る, 受領する ②迎える, 迎え入れる
- **record** 名 記録, 登録, 履歴 動 記録 [登録] する
- **red** 形 赤い 名 赤, 赤色
- **Red Cross** 赤十字社
- **red-and-white-checked pattern** 赤と白のチェック模様が入っている
- **register** 動 登録する
- **relationship** 名 関係, 関連, 血縁関係
- **relative** 名 親戚, 同族
- **religion** 名 宗教, ~教, 信条
- **religious** 形 ①宗教の ②信心深い
- **remain** 動 ①残っている, 残る ②(~の) ままである [いる]
- **remember** 動 思い出す, 覚えている, 忘れないでいる
- **reminder** 名 思い出させるもの
- **reply** 動 答える, 返事をする, 応答する
- **report** 動 ①報告 [通知・発表] する ②記録する, 記事を書く 名 ①報告, レポート ②(新聞の) 記事, 報道
- **respect** 名 ①尊敬, 尊重 ②注意, 考慮 動 尊敬 [尊重] する
- **responsibility** 名 ①責任, 義務, 義理 ②負担, 責務
- **rest** 動 休む, 眠る
- **retreat** 動 後退する, 退く
- **return** 動 帰る, 戻る, 返す
- **rich** 形 ①富んだ, 金持ちの ②豊かな, 濃い, 深い
- **ride** 動 乗る, 乗って行く, 馬に乗る 名 乗ること
- **right** 形 ①正しい ②適切な 副 ①まっすぐに, すぐに ②ちょうど, 正確に right away すぐに
- **Rin Tin Tin**「名犬リンチンチン」《映画》

WORD LIST

- **rise** 名 ①上昇, 上がること ②発生
- **rob** 動 奪う, 金品を盗む, 襲う
- **robber** 名 泥棒, 強盗
- **robbery** 名 泥棒, 強盗
- **Robert** 名 ローベルト《オットーの兄》
- **rode** 動 ride(乗る)の過去
- **room** 名 ①部屋 ②空間, 余地 dining room 食堂
- **roommate** 名 ルームメイト, 部屋を共有する相手
- **Rotterdam** 名 ロッテルダム《アムステルダムに次ぐオランダにある第2の都市》
- **row** 名 (横に並んだ)列 a row of 1列の〜
- **royal** 形 王の, 女王の, 国立の
- **ruin** 動 破滅させる
- **rule** 名 ①規則, ルール ②支配 動 支配する
- **run** 動 走る run away 走り去る, 逃げ出す run into 〜に駆け込む, 〜の中に走って入る
- **rush** 動 突進する, せき立てる rush off 急いで出て行く
- **Russian** 名 ロシア(人・語)の 名 ①ロシア人 ②ロシア語

S

- **sad** 形 ①悲しい, 悲しげな ②惨めな, 不運な
- **sadly** 副 悲しそうに, 不幸にも
- **safe** 形 安全な, 危険のない
- **safety** 名 安全, 無事, 確実
- **said** 動 say(言う)の過去, 過去分詞
- **sale** 名 販売, 取引, 大売り出し
- **sales book** 売上台帳
- **same** 形 ①同じ, 同様の ②前述の the same 〜 as … …と同じ(ような)〜 副《the –》同様に
- **sang** 動 sing(歌う)の過去
- **sank** 動 sink(沈む)の過去
- **sat** 動 sit(座る)の過去, 過去分詞
- **satisfied** 形 満足した
- **Saturday** 名 土曜日
- **save** 動 ①救う, 守る ②とっておく, 節約する
- **saw** 動 see(見る)の過去
- **say** 動 言う, 口に出す have something to say 言いたいことがある say goodbye to 〜にさよならと言う
- **scale** 名 はかり
- **scarf** 名 スカーフ
- **school** 名 学校, 校舎, 授業(時間)
- **schoolbook** 名 教科書
- **schoolwork** 名 学校の勉強
- **search** 動 捜し求める, 調べる
- **second** 名 第2(の人[物]) 形 第2の, 2番の
- **second-biggest** 形 〜に次いで大きな
- **secret** 形 秘密の, 隠れた 名 秘密, 神秘
- **secretary** 名 秘書, 書記
- **secretly** 副 秘密に, 内緒で
- **see** 動 ①見る, 見える, 見物する ②(〜と)わかる, 認識する, 経験する ③会う ④考える, 確かめる, 調べる ⑤気をつける see 〜 as … 〜を…と考える
- **seem** 動 (〜に)見える, (〜のように)思われる seem to be 〜であるように思われる
- **seen** 動 see(見る)の過去分詞
- **selection** 名 選択(物), 選抜, 抜粋
- **sell** 熟 sell out 売り切る
- **send** 動 ①送る, 届ける ②手紙を出す ③(人を〜に)行かせる ④《 – + 人[物など] + 〜ing》〜を(ある状

態に)する **send away** 追い払う, 送り出す, ~を呼び寄せる **send for** ~を呼びにやる, ~を呼び寄せる

- □ **sense** 名 ①感覚, 感じ ②《-s》意識, 正気, 本性 ③常識, 分別, センス ④意味 **make sense** 意味をなす, よくわかる
- □ **sensitive** 形 敏感な, 感度がいい, 繊細な
- □ **sent** 動 send (送る)の過去, 過去分詞
- □ **separate** 動 ①分ける, 分かれる, 隔てる ②別れる, 別れさせる 形 分かれた, 別れた, 別々の
- □ **September** 名 9月
- □ **serious** 形 ①まじめな, 真剣な ②重大な, 深刻な, (病気などが)重い
- □ **serve** 動 ①仕える, 奉仕する ②(客の)応対をする, 給仕する, 食事[飲み物]を出す
- □ **set** 動 ①設定する ②setの過去, 過去分詞 **set up a meeting** ミーティングを設定する
- □ **settle** 動 ①安定する[させる], 落ち着く, 落ち着かせる ②《-in ~》~に移り住む, 定住する
- □ **seven** 名 7(の数字), 7人[個] 形 7の, 7人[個]の
- □ **several** 形 ①いくつかの ②めいめいの 代 いくつかのもの, 数人, 数個
- □ **sewer** 名 下水道
- □ **shake** 動 振る, 揺れる, 揺さぶる, 震える
- □ **share** 動 分配する, 共有する
- □ **shave** 動 (ひげ・顔を)そる, 削る
- □ **she** 代 彼女は[が]
- □ **sheet** 名 シーツ
- □ **shiny** 形 輝く, 光る
- □ **shirt** 名 ワイシャツ, ブラウス
- □ **shock** 名 衝撃, ショック 動 ショックを与える
- □ **shocked** 形 ショックを受けて, 憤慨して
- □ **shoe** 名 《-s》靴
- □ **shook** 動 shake (振る)の過去
- □ **shoot** 動 (銃を)撃つ
- □ **shooting** 名 射撃, 発砲
- □ **shop** 名 ①店, 小売り店 ②仕事場 動 買い物をする **go shopping** 買い物に行く
- □ **short** 形 短い 副 短く 名 **for short** 略して
- □ **shot** 動 shoot (撃つ)の過去, 過去分詞
- □ **should** 助 ~すべきである, ~したほうがよい
- □ **shoulder** 名 肩
- □ **shout** 動 叫ぶ, 大声で言う, どなりつける
- □ **show** 動 ①見せる, 示す, 見える ②明らかにする, 教える ③案内する
- □ **shower** 名 シャワー 動 シャワーを浴びる
- □ **shy** 形 内気な, 恥ずかしがりの, 臆病な
- □ **sick** 形 ①病気の ②むかついて, いや気がさして **be sick in bed** 病気で寝ている
- □ **side** 名 側, 横, そば, 斜面 **one side** 片側
- □ **sign** 名 きざし, 徴候
- □ **silently** 副 静かに, 黙って
- □ **similar** 形 同じような, 類似した, 相似の
- □ **simple** 形 ①単純な, 簡単な, 質素な ②単一の, 単独の ③普通の, ただの
- □ **since** 接 ①~以来 ②~だから 前 ~以来 副 それ以来
- □ **sing** 動 ①(歌を)歌う ②さえずる
- □ **single** 形 ①たった1つの ②それぞれの
- □ **sister** 名 姉妹, 姉, 妹

Word List

- **sit** 動 ①座る, 腰掛ける ②止まる ③位置する **sit on** ～の上に乗る, ～の上に乗って動けないようにする
- **situation** 名 ①場所, 位置 ②状況, 境遇, 立場
- **six** 名 6 (の数字), 6人[個] 形 6の, 6人[個]の
- **sixteen** 名 16 (の数字), 16人[個] 形 16の, 16人[個]の
- **sixty** 名 60 (の数字), 60人[個] 形 60の, 60人[個]の
- **skate** 動 **ice skate** アイス・スケートをする
- **skill** 名 ①技能, 技術 ②上手, 熟練
- **skilled** 形 熟練した, 腕のいい, 熟練を要する
- **skin** 名 皮膚
- **skirt** 名 スカート
- **sky** 名 ①空, 天空, 大空 ②天気, 空模様, 気候
- **slave** 名 奴隷
- **sleep** 動 眠る, 寝る **go to sleep** 寝る **sleep in** 寝床に入る, 朝寝坊する, 住み込む **sleep well** よく眠る 名 睡眠
- **slept** 動 sleep (眠る) の過去, 過去分詞
- **slice** 名 薄切りの1枚, 部分
- **slowly** 副 遅く, ゆっくり
- **small** 形 ①小さい, 少ない ②取るに足りない
- **smell** 動 (～の) においがする
- **smiling** 形 ほほ笑んでいる
- **smoke** 名 煙, 煙状のもの
- **so** 副 ①とても ②同様に, ～もまた ③《先行する句・節の代用》そのように, そう **so ～ that …** 非常に～なので … **so many** 非常に多くの **so that** ～するために, それで, ～できるように 接 ①だから, それで ②では, さて
- **soap** 名 石けん
- **society** 名 社会, 世間
- **soil** 名 土, 土地 **on Dutch soil** オランダ領内で
- **sold** 動 sell (売る) の過去, 過去分詞
- **soldier** 名 兵士, 兵卒
- **solution** 名 ①分解, 溶解 ②解決, 解明, 回答 **final solution** 大量殺りく
- **some** 形 ①いくつかの, 多少の ②ある, 誰か, 何か 副 約, およそ 代 ①いくつか ②ある人[物]たち
- **somebody** 代 誰か, ある人 名 ひとかどの人物, 大物
- **someone** 代 ある人, 誰か
- **something** 代 ①ある物, 何か ②いくぶん, 多少 **something to do** 何か～すべきこと
- **sometimes** 副 時々, 時たま
- **son** 名 息子, 子弟, ～の子
- **song** 名 歌, 詩歌, 鳴き声
- **soon** 副 まもなく, すぐに, すみやかに **as soon as** ～するとすぐ, ～するや否や
- **sore** 名 傷, ふれると痛いところ
- **sorry** 形 気の毒に[申し訳なく]思う, 残念な
- **sound** 動 ①音がする, 鳴る ②(～のように) 思われる ③(～と) 聞こえる **sound like** ～のように聞こえる
- **soup** 名 スープ
- **south** 名 《the-》南, 南方, 南部 形 南の, 南方[南部]の
- **South Amsterdam** 南アムステルダム《地名》
- **space** 名 ①空間, 宇宙 ②すき間, 余地, 場所, 間
- **speak** 動 話す, 言う, 演説する **speak to** ～と話す
- **special** 形 ①特別の, 特殊の, 臨時の ②専門の
- **spend** 動 ①(金などを) 使う, 消費[浪費]する ②(時を) 過ごす

- □ **spent** 動 spend (使う) の過去, 過去分詞
- □ **spinach** 名 ホウレンソウ
- □ **spite** 熟 **in spite of** ~にもかかわらず
- □ **spoke** 動 speak (話す) の過去
- □ **sport** 名 ①スポーツ ②《-s》競技会, 運動会
- □ **spread** 動 ①広がる, 広げる, 伸びる, 伸ばす ②塗る, まく, 散布する
- □ **spring** 名 春
- □ **stand** 立つ, 立たせる, 立っている, ある
- □ **star** 名 ①星, 星形の物 ②人気者
- □ **start** 動 ①出発する, 始まる, 始める ②生じる, 生じさせる **start doing** ~し始める **start over** もう一度やり直す **start to do** ~し始める 名 出発, 開始
- □ **state** 名 国家, (アメリカなどの) 州
- □ **station** 名 駅
- □ **stay** 動 ①とどまる, 泊まる, 滞在する ②持続する, (~の) ままでいる **stay at** (場所) に泊まる **stay in** 家にいる, (場所) に泊まる, 滞在する **stay with** ~の所に泊まる
- □ **steal** 動 ①盗む ②こっそり手に入れる, こっそり~する
- □ **step** 動 歩む, 踏む
- □ **Stephan** 名 ステファン《アンネのいとこ》
- □ **stiff** 形 ①堅い, 頑固な ②堅苦しい **stiff fighting** 過酷な戦い
- □ **still** 副 ①まだ, 今でも ②それでも (なお) 形 静止した, 静かな
- □ **stocking** 名 ストッキング, 長靴下
- □ **stolen** 動 steal (盗む) の過去分詞
- □ **stone** 名 石, 小石
- □ **stood** 動 stand (立つ) の過去, 過去分詞
- □ **stop** 動 ①やめる, やめさせる, 止める, 止まる ②立ち止まる **stop doing** ~するのをやめる
- □ **store** 名 店 動 蓄える, 貯蔵する
- □ **storm** 動 ①襲撃[強襲]する ②突入する
- □ **story** 名 ①物語, 話 ②(建物の) 階
- □ **straight** 副 ①一直線に, まっすぐに, 垂直に ②率直に
- □ **strange** 形 ①知らない, 見[聞き]慣れない ②奇妙な, 変わった
- □ **stranger** 名 ①見知らぬ人, 他人 ②不案内[不慣れ]な人
- □ **strawberry** 名 イチゴ(苺)
- □ **street** 名 ①街路 ②《S-》~通り
- □ **strong** 形 ①強い, 堅固な, 強烈な ②濃い ③得意な 副 強く, 猛烈に
- □ **student** 名 学生, 生徒
- □ **study** 動 勉強する 名 勉強
- □ **style** 名 やり方, 流儀, 様式, スタイル
- □ **subject** 名 ①話題, 議題, 主題 ②学科
- □ **success** 名 成功, 幸運, 上首尾
- □ **successful** 形 成功した, うまくいった
- □ **such** 形 ①そのような, このような ②そんなに, とても, 非常に **such ~ that …** 非常に~なので… **such a** そのような **such as** たとえば~, ~のような
- □ **suddenly** 副 突然, 急に
- □ **suffering** 名 苦痛, 苦しみ, 苦難
- □ **sugar** 名 砂糖
- □ **suggest** 動 ①提案する ②示唆する
- □ **summer** 名 夏
- □ **sun** 名《the -》太陽, 日
- □ **Sunday** 名 日曜日
- □ **supply** 名 供給(品), 給与, 補充
- □ **support** 動 ①支える, 支持する ②養う, 援助する 名 ①支え, 支持 ②援助, 扶養

WORD LIST

- **sure** 形 確かな, 確実な, 《be – to ~》必ず[きっと]~する, 確信して **make sure** 確かめる, 確認する 副 確かに, まったく, 本当に
- **surprise** 動 驚かす, 不意に襲う
- **surprised** 動 surprise (驚かす) の過去, 過去分詞 形 驚いた **be surprised to do** ~して驚く
- **surrender** 動 降伏する, 引き渡す
- **surround** 動 囲む, 包囲する
- **survival** 名 生き残ること, 生存者, 残存物
- **survive** 動 ①生き残る, 存続する, なんとかなる ②長生きする, 切り抜ける
- **surviving** 形 存続[生存]している
- **survivor** 名 生存者, 残ったもの, 遺物
- **swim** 動 泳ぐ
- **swimming** 名 水泳
- **Switzerland** 名 スイス《国名》
- **synagogue** 名 シナゴーグ《ユダヤ教の会堂》
- **system** 名 制度, 系統, 体系, 秩序だった方法, 順序

T

- **table** 名 ①テーブル, 食卓, 台 ②一覧表
- **take** 動 ①取る, 持つ ②持って[連れて]いく, 捕らえる ③乗る ④(時間・労力を)費やす, 必要とする ⑤(ある動作を)する ⑥飲む ⑦耐える, 受け入れる **take ~ to …** ~を…に連れて行く **take a picture** 写真を撮る **take away** ①連れ去る ②取り上げる, 奪い去る ③取り除く **take apart** 分解する **take care of** ~の世話をする, ~の面倒を見る, ~を管理する **take good care of** ~を大事に扱う, 大切にする **take long** 時間がかかる **take over** 引き継ぐ, 支配する, 乗っ取る **take place** 行われる, 起こる **take up** (時間・場所を)とる
- **taken** 動 take (取る) の過去分詞
- **talent** 名 才能, 才能ある人
- **talk** 話す, 語る, 相談する **talk into** ~をするように説得する 名 ①話, おしゃべり ②演説 ③《the – 》話題
- **talkative** 形 話し好きな, おしゃべりな
- **talker** 名 おしゃべりな人
- **talking** 名 おしゃべり, 会話
- **tall** 形 高い, 背の高い
- **tattoo** 動 入れ墨をする
- **taught** 動 teach (教える) の過去, 過去分詞
- **teacher** 名 先生, 教師
- **teenager** 名 10代の人, ティーンエイジャー《13歳から19歳》
- **tell** 動 ①話す, 言う, 語る ②教える, 知らせる, 伝える ③わかる, 見分ける **tell ~ to …** ~に…するように言う
- **ten** 名 10(の数字), 10人[個] 形 10の, 10人[個]の
- **tenth** 名 第10番目(の人・物), 10日 形 第10番目の
- **terrible** 形 恐ろしい, ひどい, ものすごい, つらい
- **terrified** 形 おびえた, こわがった
- **territory** 名 ①領土 ②(広い)地域, 範囲, 領域
- **than** 接 ~よりも, ~以上に
- **thank** 動 感謝する, 礼を言う
- **thankful** 形 ありがたく思う
- **thanks** 熟 **thanks to** ~のおかげで, ~の結果
- **that** 形 その, あの 代 ①それ, あれ, その[あの]人[物] ②《関係代名詞》~である… 接 ~ということ, ~なので, ~だから **so ~ that …** 非常に~なので… **so that** ~するために, そ

THE STORY OF ANNE FRANK

- **the** 冠①その, あの ②《形容詞の前で》〜な人々 副《− + 比較級, − + 比較級》〜すればするほど…
- **theater** 名劇場
- **their** 代彼(女)らの, それらの
- **theirs** 代彼(女)らのもの, それらのもの
- **them** 代彼(女)らを[に], それらを[に]
- **themselves** 代彼(女)ら自身, それら自身
- **then** 副その時(に・は), それから, 次に **just then** そのとたんに 名その時 形その当時の
- **there** 副①そこに[で・の], そこへ, あそこに ②《− is [are] 〜》〜がある[いる] **there is no way** 〜する見込みはない
- **these** 代これら, これ 形これらの, この
- **they** 代①彼(女)らは[が], それらは[が] ②(一般の)人々は[が]
- **thin** 形薄い, 細い, やせた, まばらな
- **thing** 名①物, 事 ②《-s》事情, 事柄 ③《one's -s》持ち物, 身の回り品 ④人, やつ
- **think** 動思う, 考える
- **thinker** 名思想家, 考える人
- **third** 名第3(の人[物]) 形第3の, 3番の
- **thirteen** 名13(の数字), 13人[個] 形13の, 13人[個]の
- **thirteenth** 名第13番目(の人[物]), 13日 形第13番目の
- **thirty** 名30(の数字), 30人[個] 形30の, 30人[個]の
- **this** 形①この, こちらの, これを ②今の, 現在の **this one** これ, こちら **this way** このように 代①これ, この人[物] ②今, ここ **like this** このような, こんなふうに
- **those** 形それらの, あれらの **those who** 〜する人々 代それら[あれら]の人[物]
- **thought** 動 think (思う)の過去, 過去分詞 名考え, 意見
- **thoughtful** 形思慮深い, 考え込んだ
- **thousand** 名①1000(の数字), 1000人[個] ②《−s》何千, 多数 **thousands of** 何千という 形①1000の, 1000人[個]の ②多数の
- **three** 名3(の数字), 3人[個] 形3の, 3人[個]の
- **three-story** 形3階(建て)の
- **threw** 動 throw (投げる)の過去
- **through** 前〜を通して, 〜中を[に], 〜中 **look through** 〜をのぞき込む 副①通して ②終わりまで, まったく, すっかり **go through** 通り抜ける, 一つずつ順番に検討する **live through** (危機などを)乗り越える
- **throughout** 前①〜中, 〜を通じて ②〜のいたるところに
- **time** 名①時, 時間, 歳月 ②時期 ③期間 ④時代 ⑤回, 倍 **a hard time** つらい時期 **all the time** ずっと, いつも, その間ずっと **at the time** そのころ, 当時は **at times** 時には **by the time** 〜する時までに **by this time** この時までに, もうすでに **each time** 〜するたびに **every time** 〜するときはいつも **for the first time** 初めて **in time** 間に合って, やがて **the last time** この前〜したとき
- **tiny** 形ちっぽけな, とても小さい
- **tired** 形①疲れた, くたびれた ②あきた, うんざりした
- **to** 前①《方向・変化》〜へ, 〜に, 〜の方へ ②《程度・時間》〜まで ③《適合・付加・所属》〜に ④《− + 動詞の原形》〜するために[の], 〜する, 〜

Word List

すること
- **together** 副 ①一緒に, ともに ②同時に
- **toilet** 名 トイレ, 化粧室
- **told** 動 tell (話す) の過去, 過去分詞
- **tonight** 副 今夜は
- **too** 副 ①~も (また) ②あまりに~すぎて, とても~
- **took** 動 take (取る) の過去
- **tool** 名 道具, 用具, 工具
- **top** 形 いちばん上の
- **Torah** 名 トーラー (モーセ五書)《ユダヤ教の聖典》
- **Toronto** 名 トロント《カナダの都市》
- **touch** 動 ①触れる, さわる, ~を触れさせる ②接触する ③感動させる
- **touching** 形 人の心を動かす, 感動させる
- **tough** 形 堅い, 丈夫な, たくましい, 骨の折れる, 困難な
- **toward** 前 ①《運動の方向・位置》~の方へ, ~に向かって ②《目的》~のために
- **towel** 名 タオル
- **town** 名 町, 都会, 都市
- **train** 名 列車
- **transfer** 動 ①移動する ②移す ③譲渡する
- **transit** 名 通過, 乗り換え, トランジット
- **translate** 動 ①翻訳する, 訳す ②変える, 移す
- **travel** 動 ①旅行する, 移動する [させる]
- **treat** 動 ①扱う ②治療する ③おごる
- **trial** 名 裁判
- **trip** 名 ①(短い) 旅行, 遠征, 遠足, 出張 ②幻覚体験, トリップ
- **troop** 名 隊

- **trouble** 名 ①困難, 迷惑 ②心配, 苦労 ③もめごと get ~ into trouble ~を面倒 [トラブル] に巻き込む in trouble 面倒な状況で, 困って
- **trouble-making** 形 もめ事ばかり起こす
- **truck** 名 トラック, 運搬車
- **true** 形 ①本当の, 本物の, 真の ②誠実, 確かな come true 実現する
- **truly** 副 全く, 本当に
- **try** 動 ①やってみる, 試みる ②努力する, 努める try one's best 全力を尽くす
- **turn** 動 ①ひっくり返す, 回転する [させる], 曲がる, 曲げる, 向かう, 向ける ②(~に) なる, (~に) 変える turn away 向こうへ行く, 追い払う, (顔を) そむける, 横を向く turn in 向きを変える, (向きを変えてわき道などに) 入る, 床につく turn into ~に変わる turn to ~の方を向く
- **twelve** 名 12 (の数字), 12人 [個] 形 12の, 12人 [個] の
- **twenty** 名 20 (の数字), 20人 [個] 形 20の, 20人 [個] の
- **two** 名 2 (の数字), 2人 [個] 形 2の, 2人 [個] の
- **type** 名 型, タイプ, 様式
- **typhus** 名 発疹チフス
- **typist** 名 タイピスト

U

- **uncle** 名 おじ
- **under** 前 ①《位置》~の下 [に] ②《状態》~で, ~を受けて, ~のもと ③《数量》~以下 [未満] の, ~より下の
- **understand** 動 理解する, わかる, ~を聞いて知っている
- **understood** 動 understand (理解する) の過去, 過去分詞

- □ **underwear** 名 下着(類)
- □ **undress** 動 衣服を脱がせる, 着物を脱ぐ
- □ **uniform** 名 制服
- □ **United States** 名 アメリカ合衆国《国名》
- □ **until** 前 ～まで(ずっと) 接 ～の時まで, ～するまで
- □ **up** 副 ①上へ, 上がって, 北へ ②立って, 近づいて ③向上して, 増して be up to ～する力がある, ～しようとしている, ～の責任[義務]である up to ～まで, ～に至るまで, ～に匹敵して 前 ①～の上(の方)へ, 高い方へ ②(道)に沿って
- □ **upset** 動 気を悪くさせる, (心・神経など)をかき乱す
- □ **upstairs** 副 2階へ[に], 階上へ
- □ **us** 代 私たちを[に]
- □ **use** 動 ①使う, 用いる ②費やす 名 使用, 用途
- □ **used** 熟 get used to ～になじむ, ～に慣れる used to ①以前は～だった, 以前はよく～したものだった ②《be -》～に慣れる
- □ **useful** 形 役に立つ, 有効な, 有益な
- □ **useless** 形 役に立たない, 無益な
- □ **usual** 形 通常の, いつもの, 平常の, 普通の as usual いつものように, 相変わらず
- □ **usually** 副 普通, いつも(は)

V

- □ **vacation** 名 (長期の)休暇 on vacation 休暇で
- □ **valuables** 名 貴重品
- □ **van Gelder** ファン・ヘルデル《アンネのモンテッソーリ学校の時の先生》
- □ **van Pels** ファン・ペルス《人名》
- □ **vegetable** 名 野菜, 青物
- □ **very** 副 とても, 非常に, まったく
- □ **Victor Kugler** ヴィクトール・クーフレル《オットーの会社の従業員。ミープらと共に, フランク家の隠れ家生活をサポートする。1900–1981》
- □ **victory** 名 勝利, 優勝
- □ **visit** 動 訪問する
- □ **voice** 名 ①声, 音声 ②意見, 発言権

W

- □ **wait** 動 ①待つ,《 – for ～》～を待つ ②延ばす, 延ばせる, 遅らせる ③《 – on [upon] ～》～に仕える, 給仕をする
- □ **wake** 動 ①目がさめる, 起きる, 起こす ②奮起する wake up 起きる, 目を覚ます
- □ **walk** 動 歩く, 歩かせる, 散歩する walk along (前へ)歩く, ～に沿って歩く walk around 歩き回る, ぶらぶら歩く walk past 通り過ぎる walk to ～まで歩いて行く walk up to ～に歩み寄る 名 歩くこと, 散歩
- □ **wall** 名 ①壁, 塀 ②障壁
- □ **Walter** 名 ヴァルター《エーディトの兄》
- □ **want** 動 ほしい, 望む, ～したい, ～してほしい
- □ **war** 名 戦争(状態), 闘争, 不和
- □ **warehouse** 名 倉庫, 問屋, 商品保管所
- □ **warm** 形 ①暖かい, 温暖な ②思いやりのある, 愛情のある
- □ **wartime** 名 戦時(中)
- □ **was** 動《be の第1・第3人称単数現在 am, is の過去》～であった, (～に)いた[あった]
- □ **watch** 動 ①じっと見る, 見物する ②注意[用心]する, 監視する
- □ **water** 名 水

WORD LIST

- **watery** 形 水の(ような), 湿った, 水っぽい
- **way** 名 ①道, 通り道 ②方向, 距離 ③方法, 手段 ④習慣 **there is no way** ~する見込みはない **this way** このように **way of life** 生き様, 生き方, 暮らし方 **way of** ~する方法 **way out** 出口, 逃げ道, 脱出方法, 解決法 **way to** ~する方法
- **we** 代 私たちは[が]
- **weak** 形 ①弱い, 力のない, 病弱な ②劣った, へたな, 苦手な
- **weapon** 名 武器, 兵器
- **wear** 動 ①着る, 着ている, 身につける ②疲れる, 消耗する, すり切れる
- **wedding** 名 結婚式, 婚礼
- **Wednesday** 名 水曜日
- **week** 名 週, 1週間
- **weekend** 名 週末 **on the weekends** 週末に
- **weigh** 動 ①(重さを)はかる ②重さが~ある ③圧迫する, 重荷である
- **well** 副 ①うまく, 上手に ②十分に, よく, かなり **as well** なお, その上, 同様に **do well** 成績が良い, 成功する **sleep well** よく眠る **very well** 結構, よろしい
- **went** 動 go (行く)の過去
- **were** 動《be の2人称単数・複数の過去》~であった, (~に)いた[あった]
- **Westerbork** 名 ヴェステルボルク通過収容所《強制収容所に移送されるまでの一時収容所》
- **Weteringschans** 名 ベーテリングスハンス《アムステルダムの地名, 拘置所》
- **what** 代 ①何が[を・に] ②《関係代名詞》~するところのもの[こと] **what if** もし~だったらどうなるだろうか 形 ①何の, どんな ②なんと ③~するだけの 副 いかに, どれほど
- **when** 副 ①いつ ②《関係副詞》~するところの, ~するとその時, ~するとき 接 ~の時, ~するとき 代 いつ
- **whenever** 接 ①~するときはいつでも, ~するたびに ②いつ~しても
- **where** 副 ①どこに[で] ②《関係副詞》~するところ, そしてそこで, ~するところ **where to** どこで~すべきか 接 ~なところに[へ], ~するところに[へ] 代 ①どこ, どの点 ②~するところの
- **wherever** 接 どこでも, どこへ[で]~するとも 副 いったいどこへ[に・で]
- **whether** 接 ~かどうか, ~かまたは…, ~であろうとなかろうと
- **which** 形 ①どちらの, どの, どれでも ②どんな~でも, そしてこの 代 ①どちら, どれ, どの人[物] ②《関係代名詞》~するところの
- **while** 接 ①~の間(に), ~する間(に) ②一方, ~なのに 名 しばらくの間, 一定の時 **after a while** しばらくして **for a while** しばらくの間, 少しの間
- **whistle** 動 口笛[笛]を吹く
- **who** 代 ①誰が[は], どの人 ②《関係代名詞》~するところの(人) **those who** 代 ~する人々
- **whole** 形 全体の, すべての, 完全な, 満~, 丸~
- **whom** 代 ①誰を[に] ②《関係代名詞》~するところの人, そしてその人を
- **why** 副 ①なぜ, どうして ②《関係副詞》~するところの(理由)
- **wife** 名 妻, 夫人
- **will** 助 ~だろう, ~しよう, する(つもりだ)
- **willing** 形 ①喜んで~する, ~しても構わない, いとわない ②自分から進んで行う
- **window** 名 窓, 窓ガラス

- **wine** 名 ワイン, ぶどう酒
- **wish** 動 望む, 願う, (~であればよいと)思う
- **with** 前 ①《同伴・付随・所属》~と一緒に, ~を身につけて, ~とともに ②《様態》~(の状態)で, ~して ③《手段・道具》~で, ~を使って
- **within** 前 ①~の中[内]に, ~の内部に ②~以内で, ~を越えないで
- **without** 前 ~なしで, ~がなく, ~しないで
- **woke** 動 wake (目が覚める)の過去
- **woman** 名 (成人した)女性, 婦人
- **women** 名 woman (女性)の複数
- **won** 動 win (勝つ)の過去, 過去分詞
- **wonder** 動 ①不思議に思う, (~に)驚く ②(~かしらと)思う
- **wood** 名 ①《しばしば-s》森, 林 ②木材, まき
- **wore** 動 wear (着ている)の過去
- **work** 動 ①働く, 勉強する, 取り組む ②機能[作用]する, うまくいく 名 ①仕事, 勉強 ②職 ③作品 **at work** 働いて, 仕事中で, (機械が)稼動中で
- **worker** 名 仕事をする人, 労働者
- **world** 名《the-》世界, ~界 **all over the world** 世界中に **in the world** 世界で
- **World War I** 第一次世界大戦《1914–18》
- **World War II** 第二次世界大戦《1939–45》
- **worried** 熟 **be worried about** (~のことで)心配している, ~が気になる[かかる]
- **worry** 動 悩む, 悩ませる, 心配する[させる] **worry about** ~のことを心配する 名 苦労, 心配
- **worse** 形 いっそう悪い, より劣った, よりひどい **get worse** 悪化する 副 いっそう悪く
- **worst** 形《the-》最も悪い, いちばんひどい
- **would** 助《willの過去》①~するだろう, ~するつもりだ ②~したものだ
- **write** 動 書く, 手紙を書く **write back** 返事を書く **write to** ~に手紙を書く
- **writer** 名 書き手, 作家
- **writing** 動 write (書く)の現在分詞 名 ①書くこと, 作文, 著述 ②筆跡 ③書き物, 書かれたもの, 文書
- **written** 動 write (書く)の過去分詞
- **wrote** 動 write (書く)の過去

Y

- **year** 名 ①年, 1年 ②学年, 年度 ③~歳 **for years** 何年も **for ~ years** ~年間, ~年にわたって
- **-year-old** ~歳の(人)
- **yellow** 形 黄色の 名 黄色
- **yet** 副 ①《否定文で》まだ~(ない[しない]) ②《疑問文で》もう ③《肯定文で》まだ, 今もなお **not yet** まだ~してない, まだ 接 それにもかかわらず, しかし, けれども
- **you** 代 ①あなた(方)は[が], あなた(方)を[に] ②(一般に)人は
- **young** 形 若い, 幼い, 青年の
- **your** 代 あなた(方)の
- **youth** 名 若さ, 元気, 若者

E-CAT

English Conversational Ability Test
国際英語会話能力検定

● E-CATとは…
英語が話せるようになるためのテストです。インターネットベースで、30分であなたの発話力をチェックします。

www.ecatexam.com

iTEP

● iTEP®とは…
世界各国の企業、政府機関、アメリカの大学300校以上が、英語能力判定テストとして採用。オンラインによる90分のテストで文法、リーディング、リスニング、ライティング、スピーキングの5技能をスコア化。iTEP®は、留学、就職、海外赴任などに必要な、世界に通用する英語力を総合的に評価する画期的なテストです。

www.itepexamjapan.com

ラダーシリーズ
The Story of Anne Frank アンネ・フランク物語

2011年4月5日　第1刷発行
2025年4月12日　第9刷発行

著　者　ニーナ・ウェグナー

発行者　賀川　洋

発行所　IBCパブリッシング株式会社
　　　　〒162-0804 東京都新宿区中里町29番3号
　　　　菱秀神楽坂ビル
　　　　Tel. 03-3513-4511　Fax. 03-3513-4512
　　　　www.ibcpub.co.jp

© IBC Publishing, Inc. 2011

印刷　株式会社シナノパブリッシングプレス
装丁　伊藤　理恵
組版データ　Sabon Roman + Sabon Bold

落丁本・乱丁本は、小社宛にお送りください。送料小社負担にてお取り替えいたします。本書の無断複写（コピー）は著作権法上での例外を除き禁じられています。

Printed in Japan
ISBN978-4-7946-0070-7